THE
LATIN LOVE
ELEGY

THE
LATIN LOVE
ELEGY

Georg Luck

METHUEN & CO LTD

First published in 1959
by Methuen & Co Ltd
11 New Fetter Lane, London E.C.4
Second edition 1969
© Georg Luck 1959 and 1969
Printed in Great Britain by
R & R Clark Ltd
Edinburgh

SBN 416 14230 3 Hardback
SBN 416 29930 X Paperback

Distributed in the U.S.A.
by Barnes & Noble Inc.

TO

Arthur Darby Nock

Contents

Preface to First Edition

The Latin love-elegy has been a little neglected. Other forms of literature in Rome have been studied in their historical development. There are good monographs on the Roman satire, the comedy, historiography and oratory, to mention only a few. But since W. Y. Sellar wrote his two volumes on the *Roman Poets of the Augustan Age*, no book-length study has been devoted to the elegiac poets. And even in Sellar's admirable book (Oxford 1891), they had to share a volume with Horace – as if those charming but undisciplined young men could not really be trusted to go out unaccompanied.

In more recent years, Catullus, Tibullus, Propertius and Ovid have found editors, translators and appreciative critics. It seems legitimate to consider them once more as a group because they felt themselves to be the members of one, because their work is part of the social fabric of their time, reflecting its literary climate, its manners and religious beliefs, and because they have left us a body of poetry which is a substantial hostage against oblivion.

The present book does not claim to offer an exhaustive treatment of the Latin erotic elegy. Certain problems which would require long chapters (the relationship of the elegy to drama and rhetoric, for example; or biographical and chronological questions) have only been outlined. Many of the poems with which this book deals are so fragile or so flimsy that they could easily be smothered by the weight of all-too-thorough investigations.

The student of ancient literature deals with texts. It is his business to establish and interpret these texts in order to conjure up a distant period with its manner of thought, its modes of expression, its habits and even its prejudices. If the texts happen to be official records or private documents, such as letters or inscriptions, the task of the scholar who presents them is defined rather closely by technical considerations. But if the texts with which he is concerned have become a part of world literature, his task transcends the limits of purely technical competence. He should at least venture to find the secret of their appeal. Why is Vergil still read? Why is Propertius a 'modern' poet? These questions should be answered not in a purely subjective vein, not in the manner of a personal confession, but with all the resources of scholarship.

The present introduction to the Latin elegy does not replace the standard works of reference, and it dispenses by no means with a close reading of the texts. Most of the passages quoted I have translated, because a translation often helps to bring the ancient text a little closer to us. But every translation is an interpretation. Unless the translator is a poet himself, it is safer for him to be as literal as possible and to sacrifice, if necessary, the elegance of poetic diction to a faithful rendering which does not have to be colourless for that reason.

In a sense, the reader has to do the work all over again. The theories set forth must be tested, the value-judgements need a modification here and there. But if the book, as a whole, helps to revive the interest in the Latin elegy, it has fulfilled its purpose.

Arthur Darby Nock, my teacher and friend, has examined the manuscript and contributed many valuable suggestions. It is dedicated to him as a small token of my gratitude and admiration, and in memory of the years when I was his neighbour at Harvard.

I am anxious to acknowledge the generous help of Mrs William Bates Greenough, Jr, of Providence, Rhode Island, who has read the manuscript, corrected numerous errors and copied the last draft.

For all the assistance and encouragement which I received from my wife, Harriet Richards Greenough Luck, I am deeply grateful.

Mr Alan Ker of Trinity College, Cambridge, has done a great deal to make this book more accurate and readable; I should like to thank him for his stimulating criticism.

G. L.

Bern, *Spring* 1959

Preface to Second Edition

Since the first publication of this book, in 1959, a good deal of work has been done in the field. I see some definite progress, but if I were to embody it all in this new edition, the book would lose its character and become an entirely different kind of work. Therefore, I have changed little. In Chapter 2 I have replaced the section on the elegiac couplet by a note on the meaning of the term 'elegy', and at the beginning of Chapter 4, I have rephrased the remarks on the *Vita Tibulli* and the epigram of 'Domitius Marsus'. A few notes on the history of the love elegy after Ovid have been added at the end, and the bibliography has, of course, been expanded and brought up to date. There are some other changes, partly suggested by reviewers and friends.[1]

A German edition of the *Latin Love Elegy* was published in 1961 by the Carl Winter Universitätsverlag, Heidelberg. In it I made some major changes. To mention only two: Following Knoche, Lee and Axelson I put Lygdamus into the first century A.D. This is still highly controversial. I also added a detailed interpretation of Ovid, *Amores* 3.12 in which I tried to show that the poet gives to the name *Corinna* a double meaning. He is speaking of his mistress, but he also refers to the success of his first collection of love-poems which was published under the title *Corinna*. This idea seems to have convinced few readers. Though I still believe it to be valid, I did not want to introduce it here, because it is too speculative, and it seems sufficient to have submitted it once.

For some other changes I should like to refer the reader to Professor Will Richter's thorough examination of both books in

[1] I am particularly grateful to Cyril Connolly, E. J. Kenney, A. G. Lee, Michael C. J. Putnam and L. P. Wilkinson. The criticism of K. C. Quinn has helped me to rewrite the beginning of Chapter 4. Once more I wish to thank my wife, Harriet Luck, and her mother, Dorothy Greenough, for encouragement and advice.

Göttingische Gelehrte Anzeigen (1963), 176ff, and to Professor Jean Préaux' reviews in *Antiquité Classique* (1960), 475ff and (1962), 359f.

To begin with a negative statement – no fragment of a Hellenistic love-elegy has been found. It still looks as though the Alexandrian poets had preferred to express their more personal feelings in epigrams, though the epigram may seem to us a more conventional literary form than the elegy (see my lecture on 'Witz und Sentiment im Epigramm', in: *Entretiens*, publ. by the Fondation Hardt, 1969). Thus, the weighty commentary on the rests of Meleager's *Garland* by A. S. F. Gow and D. Page (Cambridge 1965) is an important contribution to our knowledge of Hellenistic love poetry (see my review in *Göttingische Gelehrte Anzeigen*, 1967, 23–61).

It has been said that our customary distinction between 'subjective' and 'objective' love poetry was meaningless for ancient writers (A. Rostagni, in: *Entretiens*, 1956, 79ff; J. Krókowski, *Eos*, 1964, 212). Propertius sees Callimachus and Philetas as his predecessors, and Gallus is grouped together with Tibullus and Ovid. This may be so, and yet it seems strange that no Alexandrian elegy that would resemble a poem of Propertius' *Monobiblos* has come to light.

At one point during the discussions on the Greek epigram held at Vandœuvres in the summer of 1967, Professor Dihle suggested that there may have been a considerable body of 'subjective' love poetry in Greece in the late fifth and in the fourth century B.C. This could have been the reservoir (nourished by classical poetry) from which Alexandrian and Roman poets alike drew their material. The Alexandrians broke it up into the small form of the epigram, while the Romans kept the elegiac form, aiming, at the same time, for the artistic perfection of the Alexandrians. This is just a theory, but it might explain some of the problems that keep puzzling scholars. Similarly, I think, there may have been a large body of pre-classical funeral laments in elegiac form, for Hellenistic grammarians still seem to know that this had, originally, been the function of the elegy.

The role played by women in Roman society is certainly one of the reasons why Roman elegiac poetry is so unique. This has been made clear by two recent books which supplement each other: J. P. V. D. Balsdon's *Roman Women* (London 1962) and Sara Lilja's *The Roman Elegists' Attitude to Women* (Helsinki 1965). But the evidence of the poets is ambiguous. They are not reliable witnesses, as far as history and sociology are concerned, and what they say about their love cannot always be taken seriously. The literary conventions, the rhetorical exaggerations, the faded metaphors of the language of love (being her slave, being wounded by her, dying at her feet) must be discounted. Much depends on the mood of the moment and we should by no means generalize. When Ovid says (*Tristia* 2. 354)

> *vita verecunda est, Musa iocosa mea,*

he implies that the poet can identify himself at any moment with the *ego* of his poems, but that can also disassociate himself at any moment. There is always this tension between the urge to be playful and the wish to express deep feelings, between pathos and entertainment, sometimes in the same poem, more often in neighbouring pieces. When an elegiac poet is serious, he comes close to being sentimental; when he wants to be gay, he sometimes comes close to being farcical.

To ask which of the three elegists loved his mistress most sincerely does not seem to be a meaningful question. Hermann Fränkel thinks, it was Ovid; Karl Büchner declares it was certainly not Ovid. But can we still verify the depth of their love after so many centuries? We lack the material, and the criteria. It is legitimate to say, as W. Y. Sellar did, that Tibullus appears to be more tender, more affectionate, less selfish than Propertius. But can we go beyond this and affirm that he loved Nemesis more passionately than Delia?

The only thing that the elegiac poets take seriously is their art. But when they call their poems *nugae*, *lusus*, they understate the hard work which these 'trifles' cost them. Propertius wishes to present only three accomplished elegies to the queen of the underworld (2.13 B); this is the ambition of the true artist.

An important influence which shaped the neoteric poets as well as the Augustans is the century in which they lived. Catullus' distichs are, perhaps, less elegantly built than those of Callimachus, but they have more emotional force and vigour. It is not the same whether one lives in third-century Alexandria or in first-century Rome. The civil wars, the rise of Caesar, the tension and general unrest of the period – all this has left traces in the work of the Roman poets, because it has formed their character. Even though Ovid was born before Actium, and does not belong to those who have, in Tacitus' words (*Annales* 1. 3. 7) 'still seen the republic', his father did. The attitude of the elegiac poets towards politics and warfare deserves a closer study. I have said too little about this in my book. Propertius' refusal to write a heroic epic, Tibullus' dislike of military service, Ovid's non-commitment – these are highly significant reactions.

Tibullus may have composed 2.5 in 17 B.C. and died shortly afterwards (W. T. Avery, *Class. Journ.* 1960, 205ff; E. Bickel, *Rhein. Mus.* 1960, 205ff), but I think he had time to arrange and publish the whole of Book 2 before he died, although its arrangement is sometimes considered the careless work of a posthumous editor. Ovid calls (*Amores* 3.9.32) Delia *primus amor* and Nemesis *cura recens*. The latter expression does not only mean 'a new love', but also 'a new book' (cf. *ex Ponto* 2.4.16).

We owe to J. P. Elder an admirable essay on Tibullus' art (see Bibliography). He shows convincingly how a kind of legend has been built up around the poet. It is true that Tibullus deliberately cultivated the 'slender style' of the Alexandrians, but that does not make him an anemic 'dabbler in winsome sweetness' (Elder, p. 70). He is a poet of 'quietly firm and independent views' (*ibid.*) who knows what he wants to say and make no concessions to fashions in politics or art. I find Elder's remarks on the pastoral element in Tibullus particularly illuminating and recommend his essay as a charming and learned introduction to a poet who has been persistently misunderstood.

Tibullus' interest in religion appears in a new light since the publication of the oath of a priest from a papyrus by R. Merkelbach and L. Koenen (*Zeitschrift f. Papyrologie u. Epigraphik* 2, 1968, 7ff) who have illustrated it with passages from the poet.

Propertius has probably had most of the benefit from the renewed interest in the Latin elegy. The commentaries of W. A. Camps (Book 1: 1961, Book 2: 1967, Book 3: 1966, Book 4: 1965) are models of succinct critical exposition and have helped immensely to elucidate the text. Propertius is a difficult poet, but there is absolutely no excuse for anyone to call him 'slovenly', as Mr K. Quinn (*Latin Explorations*, 1963, 130) has done.

It would be a mistake to read Propertius' elegies as if they were biographical documents, but certain facts emerge quite clearly. It is generally held that Cynthia was an ordinary *meretrix*, but although she may have behaved like one, she surely belonged to a distinguished family. Passages such as 2.6.1ff; 16.12 are inconclusive. On the other hand, it is impossible to deduce from 3.20.8 that one of Cynthia's ancestors was a famous poet, because the whole elegy is addressed to another woman. But 1.16 proves, I believe, that Cynthia was either of noble descent herself or married to a gentleman. Although Propertius mentions no name, the lady who lives in that old house is obviously Cynthia, for in one of his farewell poems to her, 3.25.9f

> *limina iam nostris valeant lacrimantia verbis,*
> *nec tamen irata ianua fracta manu,*

he echoes 1.16.13f (the door is speaking)

> *has inter gravius cogor deflere querelas*
> *supplicis a longis tristior excubiis,*

and 37f (the lover is speaking)

> *te non ulla meae laesit petulantia linguae*
> *quae solet irato dicere torta ioco.*

It has been pointed out that the farewell poems 3.24 and 25 resume several themes of Book 1 in the form of a *recantatio*; it should also be said that Propertius, so many years after having written his *paraklausithyron*, lifts the veil and reveals the secret of the identity of the *semper amans* (1.16.47) and the cruel lady who lives in the house.

Propertius has a peculiar sense of humour, though it is difficult to define it. Humour is, perhaps, the most elusive ingredient of literature. There are poets who have absolutely none, and when they try hard to be jocular, the result can be disastrous. But in the work of the greatest writers – and Propertius is one of them – we enjoy the radiant, irrational, effervescent play of irony and wit.

Let me quote as an example 2.29, a poem which is often

misinterpreted. Late at night, the poet walks all alone through the dark deserted streets of Rome. He is not too sober, and he has not spent the evening with Cynthia who waited in vain for him at home. Suddenly, a band of Cupids, carrying bows, arrows and torches surrounds him, stops him and puts him under arrest, at Cynthia's explicit orders (v. 9):

hunc mulier nobis irata locavit.

Although they seem to know a good deal about him and the kind of life he leads (v. 8),

iam bene nostis eum,

they let him go with a stern warning. Who are these Cupids? Of course no street robbers, as Rothstein and others have thought. Robbers have no torches and do not carry out the orders of jealous ladies. They are policemen. Propertius is well known to the Roman police, because this is not the first time that he walks through the streets of the city at a time when decent citizens are in bed. The whole poem is full of self-irony, but one has to understand the allusions in order to appreciate it.

Even in Propertius' incomparable elegy 4.7 there seem to be humorous undertones. Goethe's friend von Knebel, the graceful translator of Lucretius and Propertius, found 'flimsy, comical images' in this poem, blended, he thought, with 'expressions of deep tenderness and genuine sorrow'. It is easy to see what he meant, but difficult to put it into words. There is, in this poem, a peculiar mood that cannot simply be labelled 'humorous'. It conjures up images of the past and recaptures the lost years of a great love with all its bitterness and delight.

Philetas once described the poet as

ἐπέων εἰδὼς κόσμον καὶ πολλὰ μογήσας
μύθων παντοίων οἶμον ἐπιστάμενος
(fr. 10 Powell)

and Propertius probably applied this description to himself. The 'hellenistic' features of Book 4, as pointed out by W. A. Camps, may serve as an illustration:

(a) the poet as a guide to a visitor (4.1; cf. Catullus 4)
(b) the mentor who warns the poet against attempting a

certain kind of poetry (4.1.71ff; cf. Callimachus, Prologue to *Aitia*)
(c) the statue of a god who imparts information (4.2; cf.
Tibullus 1.4; Callimachus, *Iambs* 7 and 9)
(d) the curse poem (4.5; cf. Callimachus, *Ibis*)
(e) the poet as officiant in a ceremony (4.6; cf. Callimachus,
Hymn to Apollo)
(f) the dead person who speaks from the tomb (4.11; cf.
Anth. Pal. Book 7, *passim*).

There has been a great deal of interest recently in the structure
of Propertius' books of elegies, especially Books 1 and 4. I
mention only the articles of O. Skutsch (*Class. Philol.* 1963,
238f), W. R. Nethercut (*Am. Journ. Philol.* 1968, 449ff) and
E. Courtney (*Phoenix* 1968, 250ff). Some of the ideas and points
of view suggested in these articles seem to me valid. No doubt
the Romans had a strongly developed sense of symmetry, and
they planned their books of poetry along architectonic lines, so
that the whole collection, not only the individual poem, was a
work of art. But the more complicated the pattern becomes, the
less plausible it seems, because it imposes an almost metaphysical necessity on the arrangement of a number of poems and
tends to disregard the freedom of artistic creation.

Ovid's *Carmina Amatoria* have been edited admirably by E. J.
Kenney, and A. G. Lee has not only produced a smooth and
graceful translation of the *Amores*, but also an important essay
(see Bibliography). He shows that the three elegists are working
within a common tradition, that they rely on common conventions and then proceeds to define Ovid's individuality as a
writer: 'It is Ovid's intelligence that is individual, not his sensibility (if one can separate the two).' He rightly stresses the
pleasure the poet takes in composing and quotes from the
epistles *ex Ponto* (3.9.21f)

> *scribentem iuvat ipse labor minuitque laborem,*
> *cumque suo crescens pectore fervet opus.*

If he can still say this of the poetry of his exile, it is true in a much
deeper sense of the works of his earlier years. The fine exuberant
ecstasy of creation is a vital experience for Ovid. And yet I think

we should not overlook the self-discipline that he imposed on himself. He may or may not be a poet of the highest order, but he did not merely 'indulge his genius'; indeed he worked hard in spite of the

quicquid temptabam dicere, versus erat.

To such a writer, technique is important, and his 'Alexandrianism' (cf. E. Paratore, in: *Studi ovidiani*, publ. by the Istituto di Studi Ovidiani, 1959) is part of his technique, but learning the technique is hard work, too. It helped him achieve a kind of perfection that no other Roman poet before or after him seems to have achieved. We admire the transparence of his thoughts and the melody of his verse, and yet we cannot help feeling that these rare and wonderful qualities mark the end of a period and may have encouraged imitators rather than gifted poets to follow him. 'La clarté parfaite n'est-elle pas un signe de la lassitude des idées?'

Bonn, *Fall* 1969   G. L.

I

Introduction

Schoolmasters have special faces for them. Catullus, whose 'brutal frankness' revealed the suffering of his tormented soul (look of comprehension and pity . . . secret sorrow), irradiated by his delightful humour (wry smile); Tibullus, all rustic grace (pass on); Propertius, difficult – h'm in every sense – precious (*moue* of distaste); Ovid – great facility, bad end; an Augustan Oscar Wilde (Universal Tension).

— CYRIL CONNOLLY in *The Sunday Times*, November 29, 1959

When we speak of an 'elegy', we usually think of a melancholy and meditative kind of poem. In ancient literature, however, an 'elegy' is defined only by its metre, by the alternating sequence of a dactylic hexameter and pentameter. This metrical pattern has a gentle, yet insistent musical quality. Propertius called it 'soft', *mollis*,[1] and Ovid compared the movement of the elegiac distich to the rise and fall of a jet of water: 'In six numbers let my work rise, and sink again in five.'[2] Elsewhere Ovid describes the personified Elegy as a beautiful woman with perfumed hair, clad in a gauzy robe. The fact that 'one of her feet is longer than the other' only adds to her charm.[3]

The earliest Greek elegies deal with a variety of themes: war, politics, the pleasures and pains of life in general, love, friendship, death. They communicate a variety of moods: joy and sadness, hope and despair, deeply personal beliefs and common thought. Such fragments as we have do not tell a story for the sake of the story; they do not compete with the epic. An early

[1] Propertius 1.7.19: *et frustra cupies mollem componere versum*; cf. 2.1.2 and already Hermesianax, quoted by Athen. 13, p. 597 F.

[2] Ovid, *Amores* 1.1.27f: *sex mihi surgat opus numeris, in quinque residat.*

[3] Ovid, *Amores* 3.1.7ff.

Greek elegy is at the same time more personal and less straight-forward than the epic; it reveals more of the poet's personality, his tastes, his experiences, his philosophy of life.

The later history of the ancient elegy is marked by two important developments. (1) In the post-classical period it is adapted more generally to mythological narratives, without losing its personal and, sometimes, highly emotional character. A legend, as told by Callimachus, represents a very colourful and exciting tissue of visual impressions and side-comments. (2) During the Augustan Age at Rome the elegy becomes the preferred medium of love-poetry.

The history of the love-elegy in Rome covers only a few decades. Catullus died shortly after 55 B.C.; Propertius' first book of elegies was published around 29 or 28 B.C.; Tibullus followed with his first book soon after; and the first edition of Ovid's *Amores* appeared shortly after 20 B.C. Within less than fifty years Latin elegiac poetry had compassed an astonishing wealth of themes and situations, styles and techniques. The Greek elegy developed slowly; it had its archaic period, its classical and post-classical age. These categories of literary history seem to lose their meaning when they are applied to the Latin elegy. Everything happened more quickly, at an almost feverish pace.

Ovid, the last of the elegiac love-poets, felt that they had all been 'members of a group', *sodales*. At the end of his funeral lament for Tibullus, he describes how the dead poet meets in the underworld the shades of Catullus and Calvus.[1] In his own autobiography, written in exile, he remembers the 'friendly circle', *convictus*, and the 'comradeship', *sodalicium*, which included himself, Propertius, and two of Propertius' friends.[2] These young men used to read their poems to each other, cultivating a common tradition, proud of being the true disciples of Callimachus and Philetas.

They knew that the life they led and the verse they wrote were not altogether respectable in the eyes of their contemporaries. Obviously they were not concerned with great religious and national issues. Sometimes they make a half-hearted attempt to defend their 'naughtiness', *nequitia*. They always seem to remember that the love-elegy is a 'playful' kind of poetry (*lusus*). This

[1] Ovid, *Amores* 3.9.16f.   [2] Ovid, *Tristia* 4.10.45ff.

half-affectionate, half-deprecatory term could be applied to lyrics, epigrams, bucolics, satires, but certainly not to tragedies and epics.[1]

Both Horace and Vergil had composed 'playful poems' in their youth, but they had gone on to more serious themes and modes in later years. Tibullus died too soon to follow their example; Propertius, in his 'Roman elegies' (Book IV), and Ovid in his *Fasti* tried to show that the elegiac metre, too, was suitable to more ambitious themes. But this was hardly more than an experiment, in the case of Propertius; and Ovid knew that he would be remembered by posterity as the 'playful author of tender love-poems', *tenerorum lusor amorum*.

The Latin elegists feel more apologetic about their way of life than about the kind of poetry they write. Like Callimachus who 'shaped his verse on a narrow lathe',[2] they claim to be conscious craftsmen. They are trying to raise the elegy to a higher rank, to distinguish it from the epigram and the light improvisation. Hence they avoid certain expressions and phrases which are frequent in the epigram (Catullus, Martial).[3] For 'kiss' they prefer *osculum*; the synonym *savium* belonged to the idiom of comedy (it is found only once, in Propertius 2.29.39).

Some poets were more fastidious than others. Propertius, for example, has many colloquialisms found also in Catullus, but not in Tibullus and Ovid. In Latin, as in many other languages, diminutives have a colloquial ring. They appear frequently, as terms of endearment, or for purely metrical reasons, in Propertius' early poems. Their number decreases in his later books, as his style tends toward the elevated and grandiose. Tibullus uses them rarely, Ovid sparingly.

Occasionally the elegiac style admits of a word that is not exactly 'vulgar', but not dignified enough for the style of the epic and tragedy; for example, *plorare*, 'to cry', instead of *flere*; and *lassus*, 'tired', instead of *fessus*. It seems that the elegiac poets hesitate to divorce their language completely from that of everyday

[1] H. Wagenvoort, '*Ludus poeticus*', now reprinted in: *Studies in Roman Literature, Culture and Religon* (1956), 30ff.

[2] Propertius 2.34.43; on the meaning of this image see Richard Bentley's note on Horace, *Ars Poetica* 441.

[3] The following remarks are based on B. Axelson, *Unpoetische Wörter* (Lund 1945), 18f, 26, 36.

conversation. They dislike using certain words that had disappeared from the spoken language long ago and were (presumably for this very reason) considered effective in epic verse. *Extemplo*, 'immediately', appears ten times in Ovid's *Metamorphoses*, but never in his love-elegies.

Compared to their great contemporaries, Horace and Vergil, the elegiac poets were always at a slight disadvantage. They were read, they had an enthusiastic and devoted audience, but they never rose to the rank of 'classical' authors. Whereas we have various sets of ancient commentaries and notes on Horace and Vergil, the text of Propertius, Ovid and Tibullus is bare of explanations. This could mean that, even in Antiquity, they were read less extensively in schools than Horace and Vergil, partly because they were felt to be less suitable *virginibus puerisque*, and partly because their range of experiences was somewhat limited.

They write about love, their love. For the first time in Roman literature, love is taken seriously. Euripides and Apollonius Rhodius had shown the power of love over a woman. Plautus and Terence had brought enamoured adolescents on to the comic stage, but treated their passion in a conventional manner. The happy ending was inevitable. The other extreme we have in Lucretius. He considers love as a threat to the Epicurean peace of mind.

In Lucretius' own time the attitude toward love in literature changes radically. The society of Catullus begins to pay attention to love and love-affairs, one's own and those of others. Is this a case of literature imitating life or life imitating literature? All the poets of the Augustan Age deal with erotic themes; even Vergil cannot conceive of his serious national epic without a love-intrigue. It is possible that there was a love-intrigue in Naevius' *Bellum Punicum*, but the extant fragments give no indication of its nature, and Vergil was free to omit it if he had found it unsuitable.

This society refused to consider marriage as a happy end, but rather as an intermediary stage, a means to an end. A legal marriage had become a short-termed association for which nothing was necessary but the free assent of both man and woman. No religious ceremonies, no legal formalities were required. It was easy to obtain a divorce. Cicero's daughter Tullia had been divorced three times when she died at the age of thirty-nine.

Maecenas' wife Terentia had, as everyone knew, intimate relations with Augustus; her husband divorced her and married her again soon afterwards; 'he had only one wife, but he got married a thousand times', Seneca remarks on their frequent quarrels and reconciliations.[1]

A Roman girl could be engaged at the age of ten and married at twelve to a man chosen by her father. When she grew up to discover the meaning of love, she was no longer free. During the early centuries of the Roman Republic, as long as Rome was a city with a predominantly Roman population, the women must have accepted this situation because it was all they knew. After Rome had risen to political power, foreigners from all parts of the Mediterranean world began to stream into the city, first as traders, visitors or prisoners of war. At the beginning of the second century B.C., many of them had taken permanent residence in the capital and were active in business, or creative in literature and the arts.

With the increase in material prosperity, a taste for new pleasures and luxuries developed. In the first century B.C., we find in Rome a large number of Greek courtesans, many of whom were cultured, well-read, and accomplished dancers and musicians. They were much sought after by the fashionable set of young men. No wonder that the more sensitive and passionate among the native Roman ladies were envious of the glitter and excitements of a different way of life and resented the tedious routine of their households.

During this last century of the Roman Republic, a curious social phenomenon takes place. Ladies of the best families begin to live a rather independent life. It is not always possible to determine whether the women we meet in the love-poetry of this period are Roman matrons or Greek freedwomen. Catullus' Lesbia was a consul's wife, but Cicero speaks with heavy sarcasm of her notorious conduct. In A.D. 19 another Roman lady, the daughter of a distinguished man, registered with the police as a public prostitute. Gallus, the statesman, soldier and poet, fell in love with a Greek freedwoman whom he calls Lycoris in his elegies. Tibullus' Delia and Nemesis may have belonged to the same class. In the case of Propertius, it is not clear whether

[1] Seneca, *Epistulae*, 114.6.

Cynthia, who lives and behaves in all respects like these other girls, was not actually of an old Roman family. 'Sulpicia, the daughter of Servius', proudly signs her love-poems with her name.

As the traditional ideals of marriage lost their meaning, man and woman alike were seeking love outside marriage. The memory of traditional values such as 'faith', *fides*, 'affection and respect', *pietas*, and 'chastity', *castitas*, were nevertheless still alive; only they were now transferred from the legal union between man and wife to the loose association between the lover and his mistress.

Tibullus paints in idyllic colours the life he wishes to lead in the country at the side of his Delia. Propertius rejoices when he hears that the Emperor has withdrawn one of his marital laws which seemed to threaten his affair with Cynthia, but he speaks of her as 'for ever my mistress and for ever my wife'.[1] In one of his late poems Catullus reminds Lesbia that he loved her 'as a father loves his children'.[2]

To these poets the 'eternal union', *foedus aeternum*, between a man and a woman no longer seems possible nor desirable within a legal marriage; it can only be realized in the ideal love-affair. Ovid swears by all the gods that he will never seek another mistress than Corinna.[3]

The elegiac poets and, later, the satirists and the Christian church fathers, convey only one side of the picture. Many private documents, such as letters and funeral inscriptions, show that among the middle and lower classes the old ideals of loyalty and affection were still alive. Augustus tried to impose them by force on the upper classes, but the conjugal laws which he proclaimed at various times after 28 B.C. met with such violent opposition that he was obliged to postpone their enforcement until A.D. 9. At about the same time, by an act of curious brutality, he showed how determined he was. He banished Ovid, the poet who had symbolized the frivolity of a whole period, on questionable charges, to the Black Sea, where he died obscurely in A.D. 17, without ever seeing Rome again. His exile marks the end of elegiac love-poetry in Rome.

[1] Propertius 2.7, 2.6.42.   [2] Catullus 72.3f.   [3] Ovid, *Amores* 3.2.61f.

2

The Origin of the Elegy as a Literary Form

. . . de tous les poëmes, j'ose dire qu'après le dramatique, il n'en est point qui soit plus propre à nous émouvoir que l'Élégie. Soit que les cheveux épars, elle gémisse sur un cercueil, soit que moins négligée, mais pourtant modeste en sa parûre, elle chante les plaisirs ou les peines des amants: jamais elle n'employe d'autre langage que celuy du cœur, & sa cadence est toûjours parfaitement convenable aux sujets qu'elle s'est proposé d'imiter.

– ABBÉ SOUCHAY, 'Discours sur l'élégie': *Mémoires de l'Académie des Inscriptions et Belles-Lettres*, vol. 7 (1733), p. 335

The origin of the elegy as a literary form is obscure. Even the Alexandrian grammarians could not decide who had been its 'inventor' ($\epsilon\dot{v}\rho\epsilon\tau\dot{\eta}s$). Some suggested Archilochus, others Mimnermus; Aristotle, in his dialogue 'On Poets', seems to have favoured Callinus. Those were obviously the authors of the earliest elegiac poems known to the Alexandrians.

> *quis tamen exiguos elegos emiserit auctor*
> *grammatici certant, et adhuc sub iudice lis est.*

'But the critics dispute who was the first to produce slender elegies – and the controversy has not yet been settled.'

(Horace, *Ars Poetica* v. 77f)

The word $\check{\epsilon}\lambda\epsilon\gamma os$ 'elegy' appears several times in the lyrical passages of Euripidean tragedies where it means invariably a 'song of mourning'. One should remember the unparalleled monody of Hector's wife (*Andromache* 103-116) lamenting her husband in elegiac couplets. In fifth-century Greek usage this seems to have been the accepted meaning of the term. Hence, later grammarians derived their fanciful etymology: ἔλεγος from ἒ ἒ λέγειν 'to cry woe! woe!'

In Rome, this etymology was accepted by many. Marcus Terentius Varro, the great Roman scholar and friend of Cicero, compares *elegia* and *nenia*, the latter being a dirge, combining lamentation and praise, sung at Roman funerals to a flute accompaniment (*Poem.* fr. 303 Funaioli). The same instrument accompanied the early Greek elegy. The word *nenia* itself, like the word ἔλεγος, may derive from a Phrygian root. Ovid calls his elegies written in exile, the *Tristia*, mourning songs performed by himself at his own funeral: *efficio tacitum ne mihi funus eat; . . . tibia funeribus convenit ista meis*, 'I achieve that my funeral rites pass not off in silence; . . . this is the flute that befits my funeral'. (*Tristia* 5.1.14; 48.) If the Romans associated *elegia* with *elogium* (the eulogy of a deceased person), it is not likely that a very clear distinction between ἔλεγος, θρῆνος, ἐπικήδειον, nenia, querimonia, laudatio funebris was made at all times. Diomedes, the grammarian who wrote in the late fourth century A.D., is anxious to assemble various definitions and etymologies of the term 'elegy', but they are all connected with mourning and lament (*Gramm. Lat.*, ed. Keil, I, pp. 484/5). He mentions the Latin elegists without being aware that these etymologies do not apply to their work at all. It seems that the Greeks themselves had abandoned meanwhile these pseudo-scholarly derivations. When Agathias Scholasticus (sixth century A.D.) speaks of ἔλεγοι (*Anth. Pal.* 4.3b.84), he means 'love-poems' and nothing else. This testimony proves, I believe, that the impact of the Latin love-elegy has helped to change the traditional meaning of the term.

But the earliest extant specimens of elegiac poetry are by no means 'songs of mourning'; they were spirited, military and convivial songs, only occasionally (as in Mimnermus, for example) meditations in a more subdued manner. For the archaic elegy, we must assume a much wider range of feelings and moods than the one occupied by the later 'elegy'. It could be performed at a variety of occasions. Even if it was originally a lament, it must from the very beginning have absorbed thoughts and feelings which revolved around life, not death; joy, not melancholy. One of the earliest elegies preserved is Archilochus' fr. 7 (D.), in which the poet mourns a disaster at sea. The poem opens, indeed, with 'lamentable miseries', but soon turns to consolation and advice.

It is quite possible, on the other hand, that ἔλεγος at first was simply a song, any song, performed to the accompaniment of the Phrygian flute. The origin of the double flute goes far back – it is depicted in Cretan paintings many centuries before Mimnermus. The high thin sound of the pipe is traditionally Phrygian. It is 'the channel of all elegiac singing – all fugitive personal moods, delights and sorrows that ever the Western world has sung' (Freya Stark). There is an Armenian word for 'reed, flute', *elegn*, which is, perhaps, related to the name of the elegy.

Elegiac poetry in ancient Greece and Rome is defined by its rhythm rather than its mood. A Latin elegy consists of a number of 'elegiac couplets'; these couplets or 'distichs' nearly always contain a single thought, a sentence rounded in itself. The pauses and breaks suggested by the meaning tend to coincide with those required by the rhythmical pattern:

> Quid mihi, Livor edax, ignavos obicis annos,
> ingeniique vocas carmen inertis opus;
> non me more patrum, dum strenua sustinet aetas,
> praemia militiae pulverulenta sequi,
> nec me verbosas leges ediscere, nec me
> ingrato vocem prostituisse foro?
> mortale est, quod quaeris, opus: mihi fama perennis
> quaeritur, in toto semper ut orbe canar.
>
> (Ovid, *Amores* 1.15.1ff)

Both hexameter and pentameter are defined by the number and order of smaller metrical units, the 'feet'; and each foot in turn is defined by the number and order of long and short syllables which it contains. For the elegiac couplet, only two feet need to be considered:

> the dactyl (D): long-short-short
> the spondee (S): long-long

Two short syllables may be counted as a long one; but since their rhythmical value is clearly different, they may not be interchanged at random.

27

A pentameter without a strong dactylic element was inadmissible. Variation and alternation are the essence of the elegiac metre; in a larger measure, hexameters alternate with pentameters; on a smaller scale, dactyls must alternate with spondees.

Hence, 'pure dactylic' hexameters of this type

D D D D D S

Isi, Paraetonium genialiaque arva Canopi

are not too frequent; and 'pure spondaic' hexameters of this type

S S S S S S

are hardly conceivable in the classical elegy because of their monotonous thumping sound. To counteract the ponderous beat of the spondaic rhythm, the fifth foot of the hexameter is normally, the second half of the pentameter always, dactylic. Thus, a Latin elegiac couplet may be of the type

D S D D D ♩♪

D S ♩ D D

carminibŭs confide bonis – ïacet ecce Tibullus:

vix manet e toto parva quod urna capit.

In the first four feet of the hexameter, sixteen combinations of D and S are possible, in the first two feet of the pentameter only four; the remaining feet in either line must be dactylic – that is to say, light and fluent – in character.

The charm of the elegiac couplet – a charm easily felt but hard to describe – may be explained in a number of ways. There is an element of surprise in the pentameter: it seems to begin like the hexameter which has preceded it,

— ◡ ◡ — ◡ ◡ — . . .

but instead of rolling along majestically, it suddenly stops and reverses, becoming its own echo. Moreover, there is an intensely 'personal' element in the pentameter: instead of reaching out to embrace the world, it hesitates, it reconsiders and ends on an abrupt final note – whose abruptness is softened immediately by the renewal of the rolling beat in the following hexameter. The break in the middle of the peutameter and the echo-like effect of its second half are highly characteristic.

Because of its symmetry, the pentameter encourages the use of internal rhyme:

> *Quid pater Ismario, quid mater profuit Orpheo?*
> *carmine quid victas obstipuisse feras?*
> *Et Linon in silvis idem pater 'aelinon!' altis*
> *dicitur invita concinuisse lyra.*

The scanty remains of the Hellenistic elegy are full of such rhymes. According to statistics, only one Latin pentameter in five shows it, but wherever it appears, the reader is immediately aware of it. Perhaps the rhymes are not always intentional, but they emphasize very strongly the skeleton of the pentameter, and they belong to a large group of sound effects which all Latin poets since Ennius applied consciously. In the passage quoted above (from Ovid's elegy on the death of Tibullus), the rhymes on *-o*, *-as*, *-is*, *-a*, together with the strange, exotic names, Orpheus, Ismarus, Linos, are almost certainly intentional. They seem to convey the sound of luxuriant, half-oriental dirges. Ovid must have remembered a famous Alexandrian poem when he wrote these lines; I think one could translate them back into Greek almost word by word, without missing much of the original.

When Catullus began to write, the elegiac metre was at least seven hundred years old. Over the centuries, a limited number of 'rules' and much larger number of refinements had been tried out by Greek poets. These rules concern the treatment of the caesura, the diaeresis, the verse-endings and many other points which cannot be discussed in this book, because they require a book for themselves. The earliest Greek texts do not give the impression of periods of trial and error, of groping experimentation. We have to turn to Greek metrical inscriptions to see the lesser craftsmen struggle with these problems. But Mimnermus' distichs move with the same effortless grace as the hexameters of Homer. Should we assume that the prehistory of the ancient elegy, lost to us in the darkness of time, was almost as long as its known history? The answer to our question lies in that mysterious zone of cultural exchange between East and West – in Asia Minor.

Metrically, the Greek elegy is an offshoot of the epic, 'each hexameter running in the epic manner, but the epic flow breaking off and starting anew in the middle of the second verse and stopping short at its end' (Paul Friedländer). The pentameter, on the other hand, has a lyrical quality. The elegiac couplet does not (that is to say, not before Callimachus) replace the epic manner, but modifies and adapts it, so it can express subjective moods and thoughts. If the hexameter marks a movement away from the singer, the pentameter indicates a return to the self; it is 'subjective' in character. But the archaic Greek elegists are not exclusively concerned with themselves. They always address their songs to someone, to a friend, a gathering, a political community, an army. These poets do not believe in art for art's sake; they acknowledge their moral, social or religious responsibilities to society, because they are aware of being, themselves, members of a group, not individuals in the sense of the Alexandrians who wrote for a small group of admirers.

Callinus, Tyrtaeus and Archilochus, the first elegiac poets we know of, have a great deal in common. They were all soldiers, and their poems deal with the life of the soldier. Both Archilochus and Callinus refer to the destruction of the Ionian city, Magnesia, in the first half of the seventh century B.C. Tyrtaeus, who led the Spartans in the second Messenian War, also lived in the seventh century. In his songs, Callinus of Ephesus encourages his countrymen to take up arms against the Cimmerians who were threatening the cities of the Ionian coast. He glorifies the hero and praises victory and death in battle. The elegiac fragments of Tyrtaeus, whose war songs were sung by the Spartan soldiers on the march, are exhortations on the themes of courage and loyalty. He demands the self-sacrifice of the individual in the service of the community: 'Let us fight fiercely for our country and our children; let us die and no longer spare our lives.' The distichs of Archilochus of Parus reveal a strong and original personality. He is aware of his double role as servant of Enyalius, the God of War, and as friend of the Muses, whose 'lovely gift' he cultivates.

The Greek elegy of the archaic and the classical period embraces a large number of themes. Semonides of Amorgus (late seventh century) wrote a history of Samus in two books of elegiacs which are lost. An elegy on the shortness of life and the vanity of human illusions, attributed to Simonides of Ceus, is probably his work. The elegies of Solon, the Athenian statesman (between 640 and 560) are moral and political diatribes, those of Xenophanes of Colophon (sixth century) attacks on the accepted values of contemporary society. Before the middle of the sixth century, when prose began to take the place of poetry, elegiac verse could be used for almost any kind of communication that was directed to a large audience.

Curiously enough, we find no real love-elegies in this period. Perhaps they were conceived only in the form of the convivial elegy. There are love-songs in the second book of the collection of Theognis. They remind one of the erotic epigrams of Asclepiades; but the poet Theognis lived in the sixth century, and the second book was compiled shortly after 400 B.C. It is important for the beginnings of Alexandrian poetry, but not characteristic of the pre-classical period.

Hermesianax of Cos, himself an elegiac poet, hails Mimnermus as his literary ancestor. He words his praise in such a manner as to suggest that Mimnermus 'discovered' the elegiac metre as the most suitable vehicle for his personal feelings:

> Μίμνερμον δὲ τὸν ἡδύν, ὃς εὕρετο πολλὸν ἀνατλάς
> ἦχον καὶ μαλακοῦ πνεῦμα τὸ πενταμέτρου.
>
> (Hermesianax, fr. 7.35f, Powell)

To Hermesianax, as well as to the other Alexandrians, Mimnermus of Colophon appeared as a 'gentle poet', one who had 'suffered a great deal' and found that the 'soft' cadence of the pentameter conveyed most faithfully his experiences.

Even if Mimnermus (second half of the seventh century) was not the 'inventor' of the elegiac couplet, he may have brought it to a new perfection. Apparently he was a professional poet and musician. Unlike Homer and the Homerids who represented the past, Mimnermus lends a voice to his own personality. His poetry reflects the highly developed and refined social life of an Ionian city at the end of the seventh century B.C. Of Mimnermus' fourteen elegiac fragments, no less than five are quotations from his *Nanno*, a verse collection dedicated to a courtesan of this name, if we are to believe the speculations of later critics. Hermesianax claims to know that Mimnermus was in love with Nanno (fr.

7.37, Powell); this means that the Alexandrians considered him as the founder of the erotic elegy.

But Mimnermus' elegiac style has very little in common with that of Propertius or Tibullus. Some of his fragments deal with historical events (fr. 12, Diehl), or mythological tales (fr. 10, D.). It is possible that, in the larger context of his poems, mythology and history served as illustrations to the poet's own experience, adding, as it were, in Propertius' manner, a new dimension to his personal emotions. It has been suggested, on the other hand, that Mimnermus merely addressed to Nanno his meditations on life and love in general; that her name lent a certain unity to a variety of themes.

Even though they deal with general subjects, those fragments always have a personal ring. Mimnermus' sensitiveness enabled him to catch the fleeting hours to which coarser temperaments are blind, and his skill translates these into airy melodious verse, in which all that exists is the impression of a single moment. It seems difficult to believe that his book was merely catalogue-poetry.

At the beginning of the *Aetia*, Callimachus compares the short poems of Mimnermus and Philetas to their longer compositions. Philetas' short narrative elegy *Demeter* ranks higher (according to Callimachus) than a certain long poem by the same author. Similarly, Callimachus adds, the whole sweetness of Mimnermus radiates from those of his works that are κατὰ λεπτόν, 'in the subtle manner' (or simply 'unpretentious'). He refers perhaps to the *Nanno*, a work that was highly admired by the Alexandrians.[1]

Hence Mimnermus' name appears, together with those of Callimachus and Philetas, in the 'canon' of the elegiac poets.[2]

---

[1] See Pfeiffer on Callimachus fr. 1, 9-12 (and 532). For a different view see A. Rostagni, in his lecture on 'L'elegia erotica latina', given under the auspices of the *Fondation Hardt* (vol. II, 1956), pp. 62ff. Callimachus describes one of Mimnermus' works as 'the Great Woman' – can this really be the *Nanno*, as Rostagni, p. 68, maintains? I see no parallel between this expression and Callimachus' well-known judgement on Antimachus' *Lyde* (fr. 398, Pf.); it suggests almost certainly a mythological heroine. The fact that a fragment from the *Nanno* is quoted in one of the Scholia to Antimachus is irrelevant.

[2] Cf. Proclus, in Photius, *Bibl.* p. 319 B; Tzetzes on Lycophron, p. 3.15 (Sch.), etc. The main representatives of the elegies are always Mimnermus, Callimachus and Philetas, sometimes preceded by Callinus. On the Alexandrian *canones* see my paper in *Compar. Lit.* 1958, 150ff.

When Propertius' friend, Ponticus, the epic poet, falls in love, Propertius recommends the reading of Mimnermus, for

> *plus in amore valet Mimnermi versus Homero :*
> *carmina mansuetus lenia quaerit Amor.*

'In love, the line of Mimnermus is worth more than Homer; Love (being a) civilized (deity) requires gentle poems.'

(Propertius 1.9.11-12)

To Propertius and his friend, Mimnermus is the typical representative of the erotic elegy.

Around 400 B.C. Antimachus of Colophon wrote a long narrative elegy. When his wife, Lyde, died, he tried to find comfort in ancient legends that illustrated the sorrows of love, many of them doubtless half-forgotten by this time. It seems that he has actually created this particular type of the narrative elegy. We do not know whether the death of his wife was the central theme of the work. He must have mentioned it in the preface, together with his intention to comfort himself by excursions into the mythological past; does this mean that he stressed, in each case, the parallels between the death of a heroine and that of Lyde? Callimachus read and disliked the work; he called it 'a bulky piece of writing, and not polished' (fr. 398, Pf.). Catullus repeated this verdict (c.95.10) and thus probably discouraged his successors from adopting it as a literary model.

It is still an open question whether the Alexandrian poets wrote personal love-poems in the elegiac manner. The evidence is contradictory. Asclepiades, Callimachus and many others composed erotic epigrams dealing with themes and situations similar to those in the elegies of Propertius, Tibullus and Ovid. But the difference between an epigram and an elegy is not only one of size.

The Roman elegists claim to be the legitimate successors of Callimachus and Philetas. They never specify precisely what they owed to them. Was it the imagery? Unfortunately, among the many fragments of Hellenistic poetry that have been recovered, none can be certainly designated as a personal love-elegy. This may be due to chance. The Alexandrian poets were always experimenting, always striving for new effects. Mime, *chanson* and even the literary satire, it seems, are creations of the Alexandrian age. To this desire for formal innovations they added a new

C

interest in psychology. The analytical description of rare and complex emotions was one of the primary goals of their art.

All these characteristics are found in the Roman elegy. But what was new at Rome? The social conditions? A sense of the individual that the Alexandrians did not have? It is one of the commonplaces of ancient criticism that the Roman elegy renews the tradition of the Alexandrians. Quintilian (*Inst. Or.* 10.1.93), *elegia quoque Graecos provocamus*, 'in the elegy, too, we challenge the Greeks', means by *Graeci* above all Philetas and Callimachus, whom he has mentioned shortly before as the chief Alexandrian elegists. The term *provocare*, to 'challenge', suggests competition rather than mere imitation. It implies the awareness of a great tradition, an awareness that characterizes Vergil's attitude toward Homer and Horace's attitude toward the archaic Greek lyricists. But within the larger framework of this tradition there is room for innovation.

Diomedes, the grammarian (or his source), oversimplifies the question when he says (*Gramm. Lat.*, ed. Keil, I, p. 484) *elegia est carmen compositum hexametro pentametroque . . . quod genus carminis praecipue scripserunt apud Romanos Propertius et Tibullus et Gallus, imitati Graecos Callimachum et Euphoriona*, 'an elegy is a poem composed of hexameters and pentameters . . . a kind of poetry that was cultivated in Rome, chiefly by Propertius, Tibullus and Gallus, as an imitation of the Greek poets Callimachus and Euphorion.' There is no evidence that Diomedes actually read Callimachus and the other Alexandrians. It is much more probable that he based his sweeping statement on the occasional testimonies of Propertius and Ovid, who acknowledged Callimachus and Philetas as their masters. In any event, his purely metrical definition of the elegy proves that he was not interested in its structure and imagery.

Where exactly within the Greek elegiac tradition did the Romans find a starting point for their kind of love-poems? If anywhere, in Callimachus, it seems. He experimented boldly with all genres of poetry and was the recognized leader of the 'modern poets'; the catalogue of his works includes epigrams, hymns, iambi, epyllia, narrative elegies.

Some of his epigrams are love-poems, but only one of them (nr. 63, Pf.) is addressed to a woman. It is an elegant piece of work, a little conventional and playful, and hardly an erotic elegy,[1] although it anticipates a theme that reappears later in Propertius, Tibullus and Ovid.

A fragment quoted from 'the elegies' (Callimachus fr. 714, Pf.) has a more personal ring: 'It is easier to bear one's sorrow, if one shares it with a friend.' But these lines are not necessarily taken from a 'subjective' love-poem; they could be spoken by a mythological person in a narrative elegy. There is enough room for sentimental soliloquies in stories such as *Acontius and Cydippe*. Even Callimachus' so-called objective elegies are always vividly told. One almost feels that the poet takes part in the action; we seem to hear his own voice when he depicts the feelings of his heroes and heroines. Our distinction between 'objective' and 'subjective' becomes irrelevant as soon as we deal with his poetry.[2]

In the absence of any conclusive texts, we have to discuss the testimonies of Propertius and Ovid. They like to refer to Callimachus and Philetas; they call them their masters and models, and Propertius even glories in the feeling of being a Roman Callimachus. But what works of his have they actually read?

Propertius 2.34.31f, *tu satius memorem Musis imitere Philetan* | *et non inflati somnia Callimachi*, 'you had better read Philetas who is mindful of the Muses, and the dreams of Callimachus who is not turgid', refers to the beginning of Callimachus' *Aetia*, with its famous dream-motif. The first line, incidentally, may be a reminiscence of a lost work of Philetas, but it is much more likely that Propertius transferred the context to Callimachus which he

[1] I have dealt with the authorship of this epigram elsewhere; 'Callimachus and Conopion', *Class. Quart.* 49 (1956), pp. 225ff.

[2] In Euripides' tragedies heroes and heroines in distress often address themselves to nature (*Medea*, vv. 56ff, *Ion*, vv. 870ff, etc.). When people cannot be trusted or do not understand, nature personified provides comfort. Electra laments her degradation, Iphigenia her isolation, the nurse in the *Medea* the wrong done to her. In the New Comedy, it is usually the young man in love who addresses nature (cf. Plautus, *Mercator*, vv. 3ff). This is one of the themes that the Latin elegists may have taken directly from Euripides and Menander. The whole question is important for the prehistory of the Latin Elegy. After Reitzenstein and Leo, it has been discussed by Butler-Barber in the introduction to their commentary on Propertius (1933). As it involves the influence of one literary *genus* on another, the problem is insoluble; there is always the possibility that Propertius, Tibullus and Ovid knew these dramatic themes in the form which the Alexandrian mythological elegy had given them.

had in mind to the lesser-known poet. The Muses play such a significant role in the opening of the *Aetia* that Callimachus could be properly called *memor Musis*.

Callimachus as a model of style rather than a writer of erotic poetry is further mentioned by Propertius in 2.1.39f, *sed neque Phlegraeos Iovis Enceladique tumultus | intonet angusto pectore Callimachus*, 'but neither would Callimachus be able to thunder forth, from his narrow breast, the battles between Jupiter and Enceladus on the plain of Phlegra.' This distich simply hints at the stylistic difference between the heroic epic and the Hellenistic epyllion. Callimachus avoids the time-honoured but tedious subjects, such as the *Gigantomachia*; he prefers a more intimate, more psychological approach to mythical reality, and he writes κατὰ λεπτόν, 'in the slender manner'.

But elsewhere (Propertius 3.9.43f) Callimachus suddenly appears as a love-poet: *inter Callimachi sat erit placuisse libellos | et cecinisse modis, Coe poeta, tuis*, 'enough for me to have found acceptance among the books of Callimachus and to have sung in strains like yours, poet of Cos.' This must be an allusion to Callimachus' (and Philetas') love-poetry, for Propertius continues: *haec urant pueros, haec urant scripta puellas, | meque deum clament et mihi sacra ferant!* 'Let these writings inflame the boys, let them inflame the girls, and let them acclaim me as a god and bring me sacrifice.' Again, this sort of love-poetry may well have been mythological and narrative, not subjective and lyrical. If the poet's ego entered into it at all, it did so in a veiled form. A human experience was presented through a legend; the poet himself was hiding behind his persons.

Finally, at a crucial point in his career, hesitating between the epic and the elegy, Propertius turns to the deified *Manes* of Callimachus and Philetas for advice: *Callimachi Manes et Coi sacra Philetae, | in vestrum, quaeso, me sinite ire nemus*, 'shades and sacred rites of Callimachus and Philetas of Cos, pray let me enter your grove.' The whole poem, with its religious imagery significantly placed at the beginning of a new book, shows Propertius as a worshipper of the two eminent Alexandrians. The following questions – 'Tell me, in what cave did you, side by side, refine your song? With what foot did you enter it? Or what water did you drink?' – suggest again that Propertius was mainly concerned with their style and metre rather than their subject matter (Propertius 3.1.1-6).

To sum up, whenever Propertius mentions Callimachus he sees in him either a model of style, or the elegiac poet, or (at least once) a love-poet in the vaguest sense of the word. In the catalogue of his Roman predecessors (2.34.85ff) Propertius adds to the name of each poet (Varro, Catullus, Calvus, Gallus) that of his 'mistress' (Leucadia, Lesbia, Quintilia, Lycoris). He never implies that Callimachus was in love with a woman whose name he could have made immortal by his verse. This is an important distinction.

From Ovid's occasional references we know that erotic themes had their place in Callimachus' verse. He groups the Alexandrian poet together with Anacreon and Menander (*Ars Amatoria* 3.329ff) declaring that having read them is part of a girl's social graces. Conversely, it is better not to read Callimachus and Philetas if one wants to fight a fatal amorous attachment (*Remedia Amoris* 759f), for Callimachus is *non . . . inimicus Amori*, 'no enemy to Love'.

Callimachus is listed among the erotic poets in Ovid's self-defence, *Tristia* 2.367f, 'nor did it injure you, son of Battus, that you yourself often confessed your pleasures to the reader in verse.' There is some emphasis on Callimachus' personal experience; the verb 'to confess' no doubt implies an intimate sort of poetry. Did Ovid think of the epigrams; or the *Iambi*, with their sophisticated ribaldry? Or did Callimachus actually write subjective love-poems in the elegiac manner? Ovid once remarks that his *Amores* were favourably compared to Callimachus' poetry (*Amores* 2.4.19f); but the point of the comparison may have been the technique, the style, not necessarily the themes and situations: *est quae Callimachi prae nostris rustica dicat | carmina . . .* 'there is a girl who considers Callimachus' poems rustic compared to mine. . . .'

The conclusion is still negative. Whatever Callimachus' influence on the Latin elegiac poets may have been – and it should not be underestimated – he became more and more a 'great name', a 'classic' whom one praised almost mechanically. Callimachus had started out as a rebel against literary conventions, only to establish new ones. Callimachus *may* have written personal love-elegies, but if there was one thing he could not supply, it was the fresh experience that makes the Latin elegy what it is.

Philetas of Cos, born around 340 B.C., was a scholar and a poet, like Callimachus, and one of the *principes elegiae*, the 'main representatives' of the Alexandrian elegy. Although the Latin elegiac poets praise him almost as often as Callimachus, they may have known him chiefly by reputation. At the time when Parthenius compiled his mythological love-stories for Cornelius Gallus, Philetas was little more than a great name.[1]

Still, Propertius insists that it was the 'water of Philetas' that made him an elegiac poet himself. In a dream he sees himself on Mount Helicon, near the Hippocrene, ready to follow Ennius' example and drink from those mighty fountains. Both Apollo and Calliope warn him; he is not destined to be an epic poet. To lend emphasis to her words, the Muse moistens Propertius' lips with *aqua Philetaea* (Propertius 3.3.51f).

This water is not drawn from Hippocrene, but from the 'Gorgon pool' (3.3.31f), a little lake situated nearby and, as its name implies, connected with the Hippocrene. It is a pool, not a spring. It is the same water that inspires the epic poets higher up; but now it forms a quiet little lake in which doves, 'the birds of my lady Venus, my favourite company', dip their purple beaks.

Propertius' imagery shows that he is thinking of himself as Philetas' successor. The idyllic scenery, the decorative bric-à-brac, the presence of doves – all this means that he considered Philetas as a love-poet. At the end of her speech, just before she moistens Propertius' lips with 'water of Philetas', the Muse urges him to deal with erotic themes (vv. 47-50). To Propertius these were the themes that Philetas dealt with.

Hermesianax and Ovid claim to know that Philetas was in love with a lady by the name of Bittis. He writes to his wife from Tomis: 'Not so great was the love of the poet of Clarus (Antimachus) for Lyde or that of her poet of Cos for Bittis as the love

---

[1] The fact that very few fragments of Philetas have been found on papyri seems to indicate that he was not read as widely as Callimachus during the Augustan Age. His role, as R. Pfeiffer, *Journ. Hellen. Stud.* 75 (1955), 71f, has recently suggested, was that of a pioneer. As far as we know, the designation 'a poet as well as a scholar' was first applied to him. Through his influence as a writer of elegies, short epics, and epigrams, but also as a learned collector and critic, the ideal of the *poeta doctus* took shape during the following century.

that clings in my heart for you, my wife . . .' (*Tristia* 1.6.1-3).
And in one of his later letters (*Epistulae ex Ponto* 3.1.57f), he
says: '(thanks to my writings) you have a name not inferior to
that of Coan Bittis.' Ovid promises immortality to his wife; but
she is not the Corinna of the *Amores*. His wife will be remembered as the person she was in real life, *coniunx Nasonis*, not as the
fictitious heroine of a book of love-poems. If Bittis was Philetas'
wife, she was neither Corinna nor Cynthia.

Philetas' works included epigrams as well as elegies. One of
these elegies, *Demeter*, a narrative poem, was considered by Callimachus as a model of its kind. Some of his shorter pieces (including, perhaps, light erotic epigrams) he published under the
title *Paignia*, 'playful poems'. Its Latin equivalent would be *lusus*
or *nugae*. Propertius uses *ludere*, 'to play', when he refers to the
composition of love-poems (Propertius 2.34.85); but we should
hardly expect to find Philetas' poems for Bittis in his *Paignia*.

So far we have established three facts: (1) Philetas wrote
narrative poetry in the elegiac manner; (2) he wrote poems that
dealt with love (Ovid, *Ars Amatoria* 3.329f; *Remedia Amoris* 759f),
which may or may not have been based on personal experience;
(3) he was in love with a woman whose name he made famous by
his verse. No matter how much of Philetas they had actually read,
Propertius and Ovid knew this much *about* him. If they did know
him from first hand, they found in his poetry a note of melancholy,
a sense of loss. A few deftly executed picturesque descriptions
(for example, the vision of the shady plane tree under which he
sits, confiding his grief to nature) relieve the monotony of his
sentimental and erudite manner.

Euphorion of Chalcis was born in 276. He studied philosophy
in Athens and died as a librarian at the court of Antiochus the
Great. At Rome he was known as an elegiac poet. The com-
mentator Probus notes on Vergil's *Eclogues* (10.50): 'Euphorion
was a writer of elegies from Chalcis, whose manner of writing
Cornelius Gallus seems to have adopted', *cuius in scribendo secutus
colorem videtur Cornelius Gallus*; but his influence extended to the
whole school of the *poetae novi*, the 'modernists', at Rome.
Cicero calls them sarcastically *cantores Euphorionis*, 'minstrels à la
Euphorion' (*Tusc. Disp.* 3.45).

Hermesianax, a student and friend of Philetas, made another

significant contribution to the history of elegiac poetry. He collected stories of women who had been beloved by famous poets
and philosophers and cast them into elegiac metre. Since the
situations were always the same, the book tended to be monotonous – a danger which even so skilful a story-teller as Ovid has
not always avoided in the *Heroides*. Picturesque details had to be
added to recommend the work to fastidious Greek readers.

The typical situation in Hermesianax – the poet in love – is
precisely the situation of Propertius, Tibullus and Ovid. What is
presented as a mythological narrative in the Alexandrian poet
reappears as personal experience in the Roman elegists. Naturally, the elegiac manner, with all its precious unspoken subtleties,
made any epic objectivity unnecessary or even undesirable. The
poet easily identifies himself with his protagonists.

By dedicating his book to Leontion, his wife or mistress, he
added a personal element to his theme. Did he want to prove to
her that poets, at all times, have been devoted and unselfish
lovers? Or did he merely want to remind her that love had always,
in the end, been requited while he alone was longing in vain? At
all events, the legendary love-stories may have served as παρα-
δείγματα 'examples'. They were probably not told for their own
sake, but were meant to 'prove' something. The single story becomes an αἴτιον, a 'cause' in the Callimachean sense of the word.

From its very beginning the elegy serves a practical purpose.
Callinus addresses the young men of his city and urges them to be
good soldiers. Theognis tries to hold back the decline of the old
aristocratic society. The archaic elegy is hortatory in character;
it needs an audience on whose imagination it wants to act. This
hortatory character of the elegy can be observed in Catullus and
much of Propertius, especially in his earlier poems. Later, in
Tibullus and Ovid, the elegy (at least the erotic elegy) tends toward the soliloquy; only in exile, in his *Tristia* and *Epistulae ex
Ponto*, Ovid seems to rediscover the original forms of the elegiac
appeal: lament, prayer, persuasion – but almost always addressed
to a friend or a group of friends.

It is characteristic of the Alexandrian elegy that it can be
didactic and entertaining at the same time, pathetic and amusing,
objective and emotional, narrative and lyrical. The boundaries
between the 'classical' *genera* of poetry tend to disappear. The

result is a slightly hybrid creation, an artificial gem, as it were, glittering with many facets. Melancholy and erudite wit, dry facts and decorative passages follow each other without transition.

Phanocles, a contemporary of Hermesianax, wrote a series of elegies (Ἔρωτες ἢ Καλοί, *Love-stories or Handsome Boys*) on a similar theme. Like Hermesianax or Callimachus, he needs above all a pretext to unfold his erudition. But within that framework of bookish learning we find exquisite poetic passages, for example (fr. 1, Powell) the story of Orpheus' love for Calais and the poet's death. It is not told for its own sake, but serves to explain the origin of poetry on Lesbos and – the reason why the Thracian women are tattooed (they were marked by their husbands so as to be reminded for ever of their atrocious crime). As soon as the story is launched on its way, Phanocles seems to forget its immediate purpose. For a while he abandons himself to the scenery, the human situation, and to a gracefully melancholy mood. But then historical erudition claims its rights again, and the decorative freshness of the description vanishes to give room for tedious detail.

There is still another example of this Alexandrian fusion between sentimental themes and obscure mythological tales. Alexander Aetolus, who lived under Ptolemy Philadelphus and was in charge of tragic literature at the Alexandrian library, wrote a poem in which Apollo predicts the fate of various victims of unhappy love-affairs. A fragment, quoted by Parthenius (Cleoboea's criminal love for Antheus), is apparently drawn from this catalogue-poem. All we can say is that the author has made the best out of the odd situation.

We know at least the names of many more Hellenistic elegists – some of them chiefly remembered by other works (Theocritus by his bucolic poetry, Aratus by his astronomical treatise in verse, Asclepiades by his epigrams) – and some who were probably already half forgotten in Propertius' time.

Parthenius of Nicaea (first century B.C.) represents an important link between Alexandrian literature and Latin elegiac poetry. He was brought to Rome as a prisoner of war. The titles of some of his works are known; they included, for example, a mythological elegy, *Aphrodite*, and a *Dirge* on the death of his wife Arete. His taste for 'strange and out of the way stories' – he

41

shares this, of course, with many other Hellenistic poets – is evident in the collection of *Erotic Adventures* which he compiled for Cornelius Gallus. 'You will thus have at hand a store-house from which to draw material, as may seem best to you, for either epic or elegiac verse,' he writes in the preface. Some of these stories had been treated by Euphorion, and we know that Parthenius, like Gallus, had tried to imitate Euphorion's manner; it is hard to say how much of Euphorion's art is left in this compilation, but if Gallus and the other Roman elegists knew the great Alexandrians only through such prose versions, they must have missed a great deal of the original. It seems that Parthenius had a far greater influence on Roman poetry through this collection of thirty-six love-stories than through his own verse. They were no doubt the kind of *exempla* that he had found most useful for his own poetic compositions; in one of them he even quotes himself.

This rapid survey of the Greek elegy justifies, perhaps, one or two conclusions. First, it seems that the distinction between 'objective' and 'subjective' poetry is hardly relevant in the case of Alexandrian literature. Callimachus told an old story in a new manner – Propertius told his own experience in (what he thought to be) the Callimachean manner. To a modern reader this involves an enormous difference. But are the erotic adventures of Propertius, Tibullus and Ovid really so different from those of a mythological character in Hermesianax, say, or Phanocles? The Alexandrian poets introduce modern themes into the myths they tell, and the Roman elegists introduce mythical themes into the romantic tales of their own experiences.

Second, we should not expect to find the Greek 'original' of any one Propertian or Tibullan elegy. The Roman elegists were no translators, nor were they imitators in a superficial way. They were involved in a process of creative adaptation. Perhaps they could never have written their best work without the standards which they learned from their Alexandrian predecessors. But even if they did not understand them, even if they misinterpreted them, they found in their work models for their own discipline and images of the kind of perfection they wished to attain. The respect they paid to these models is significant. This is what ultimately distinguishes the 'professional' from the 'dilettante'.

It has often been said that the New Attic Comedy of Menander and its Latin adaptations furnished a large number of situations, typical characters, plots, and themes to the Latin elegiac poets. Many scholars still maintain that it is impossible to understand the role of the lover and poet in the Latin elegy without a previous study of Terence and Plautus. According to this view, most love-elegies are little more than comedy-scenes transformed into dramatic monologues. Examples of this technique are found mainly in Ovid, for example *Amores* I . 8, where a *lena*, 'bawd', – overheard by the poet himself – delivers to Corinna a lecture on how to be a successful courtesan.

The whole problem is more than a controversy between specialists; it concerns the very essence of elegiac poetry. I maintain that the influence of Menander, Plautus and Terence can be disregarded, at least in the case of Tibullus and Propertius; that there is no evidence which would force us to derive one literary *genus* from the other, and that every single love-elegy is intelligible and meaningful to us without being illustrated by parallels from the comic poets.

No one will deny that Plautus and Terence were read by the Augustans; but the reputation of the *poeta doctus* was founded on a much more extensive reading which included the Greek epic, the tragic and lyric poets, and the works of the great Alexandrians. On the book-shelf of Propertius, the editions of the comic play-wrights surely occupied only a small place next to the editions of Homer, Euripides and Callimachus. He has read Ennius, Lucretius and Catullus, but he sees in Callimachus his true literary ancestor and he considers himself as the Roman Callimachus. After having published more than half of his work, he plans a trip to Athens, in order to read, as he says, 'the witty books of Menander'; but at this time, he was already known as the lover of Cynthia, as the 'priest' who had transplanted 'Greek mysteries' to Rome.

Plautus and Terence did not address themselves to the same kind of audience as the *poetae docti* who guarded the secrets of their art and wrote only for the initiated. The playwrights wished to entertain; their comedies would appeal to the uneducated as well as to the sophisticated, because they required no particular knowledge of mythology and literature beyond what everybody knew. Propertius, on the other hand, is almost obsessed with the esoteric character of his art; like Callimachus and Horace, he draws a sharp line between himself and the *profanum vulgus* and warns all those who are not ready to receive his message to keep out of the sacred precinct of his poetry.

Moreover, the standard plots on which the comic playwrights rely bear only the slightest resemblance to the (real or imaginary) love-affairs of the elegists. With small variations, Plautus and Terence always dramatize the same story: A young man from a good family falls in love with a courtesan, but his father plans a respectable marriage for him. The procurer to whom the girl has been sold in her youth rejects the advances of the young man, because he has already promised her to a rich client. Against this double interference, the young man, assisted by a clever slave, finally wins the girl who turns out to be the daughter of respectable parents, after all, so that the marriage can take place.

The inevitable happy ending of these plays is contrary to the very nature of the elegiac love-affair. In order to maintain the role of the jealous, unrequited, eternally longing lover, Tibullus, Propertius and Ovid cannot possibly find domestic bliss. Tibullus is fond of describing the idyllic life in the country which he might enjoy with Delia, some day; but this dream does not come true, at least not in his poems, because it *cannot* come true. If it did not remain a distant dream, Tibullus would no longer be Tibullus.

Some of the stock-characters of the Graeco-Roman comedy (slaves, witches, bawds) reappear in the elegy, but they play such a subordinated role that they have hardly any influence on the course of the love-affair. They provide a little excitement or comic relief but they are by no means the dangerous antagonists who threaten to prevent the happy ending of the typical Plautine plot. We are likely to forget that slaves and procurers were characters of real life, that they still existed in Ovid's Rome and potentially carried out the same functions which the playwrights had assigned to them more than a century ago. A short stroll in the Subura at night would teach Propertius more about their doings than the comedies of Plautus which, after all, represent a different world.

The comedy, apart from its contrived ending and a few highly improbable assumptions which help to bring about the denouement, is a mirror of life. An Alexandrian critic paid the highest compliment to Menander when he exclaimed: 'O Menander – O life – which has imitated which?' The elegy has different artistic intentions; its world is more misty, less concrete. The elegy looks at life through a veil on which the colourful legends of the past are embroidered. As the situations change, the elegiac poet sees himself in different disguises; now he is Achilles, now Acontius, now Demophoon. He is never committed to the role of the rather insipid young lover of the comedy whose character hardly changes throughout the play.

The comic playwrights give us a simplified view of life; the elegiac poets present it with a wealth of complexities. To study real life, Ovid did not have to read Menander:

> *dum fallax servus, durus pater, improba lena*
> *vivent, et meretrix blanda, Menandrus erit.*

'As long as a deceitful slave, a stern father, a wicked bawd, a slippery courtesan are to be found, Menander will be read.'
> (*Amores* 1.15.17-18)

All these characters existed in Ovid's Rome as they had existed in Menander's Athens, but the poet of the *Amores* had little use for them. Has he ever given us the portrait of a stern father, one of the protagonists of the comedy, without whom there would be no plot? And are Cynthia, Delia, Corinna just 'slippery courtesans' and nothing more? The main difference between comedy and elegy can be summed up in one sentence: The *domina*, the elegiac mistress who plays such an exalted role in Latin love-poetry from Catullus to Ovid, has no prototype in Plautus and Terence. Not all of Menander's courtesans are treacherous and greedy, many are sensitive and kind-hearted, but none of them has that extraordinary mixture of cruelty and sympathy, refinement and vulgarity, unlimited capacity for love and hatred which we find, for the first time, in Catullus' Lesbia and which is, henceforth, inseparable from the *domina*. None of Terence's women is nearly as complex and self-contradictory, none has such a compelling presence as Propertius' Cynthia.

Certain characteristic elements of the Graeco-Roman comedy, such as melodramatic monologues, philosophical declamations on the stage, meditations on the power of love in general, seem to open up a larger perspective, because they transcend the direct 'imitation of life'. It is true that they reappear in the elegies of the Augustan Age, but only because they have a common ancestor: the Greek tragedy. Here we stand on firm ground. The ancient critics noticed the sharp break between Aristophanes and Menander; they decided that Menander was much closer to Euripides than to Aristophanes. We might oversimplify the matter and say that whatever is not 'imitation of life' in Menander, is a heritage of the tragedy. Once we have reached this point, we find ourselves again in the realm of the myth, far away from the mild agitations of the parlour-comedy. The comedy tends to normalize and rationalize human emotions and conflicts; elegy and tragedy tend to show these conflicts in mythical dimensions. Theophrastus' definition of tragedy – 'the circumstance of a heroic fate' – applies, in a sense, to the Latin love-elegy as well. Ovid's occasional experiments with comedy-themes are no proof to the contrary; he was the last in the line of elegiac poets and had to explore new subjects in order to maintain the public's interest in this kind of writing. In fact, his experiments help to explain why there was no longer any elegiac love-poetry after Ovid. Once the barrier between myth and reality was broken, once the sounds and sights of real life had intruded on the traditional domain of the elegiac art-form, its character was lost. By trying to infuse new life into this art-form, Ovid destroyed the mystery which Propertius and Tibullus had maintained so jealously; the twilight which they had created could not survive the dazzling fireworks of Ovid.

3

The Early History of Elegiac Poetry in Rome

Catulle, qui te legerit,
Et non amarit protinus
Amore perditissimo,
Is, credo, se ipsum non amat,
Caretque amandi sensibus,
Et odit omnis gratias.

— IONNES COTTA

The history of elegiac poetry in Rome begins with Ennius. He introduced the elegiac distich into Roman literature but did not compose any love-poems in this metre; neither did Lucilius, whose twenty-second Book of the *Saturae* contained some elegiac poems. Propertius, who was so conscious of his literary ancestors, mentions 'Father Ennius' twice (3.3.6 and 4.1.61), but only to indicate that he could not and would not compete with him in his own domain.

The first erotic poems in Rome seem to be *vers de société*, written by aristocrats to be read by other aristocrats. Five epigrams by three authors, partly preserved by Gellius (19.9), partly by Cicero (*Nat. Deor.* 1.79), are characteristic of this kind of literature. The three authors, Q. Lutatius Catulus, Valerius Aedituus and Porcius Licinus, were still read – perhaps only in an anthology – and highly praised in the second century A.D.

It is doubtful whether any of them had a strong influence on the beginnings and development of the love-elegy in Rome. Theirs are adaptations of Hellenistic motifs, some of which may reappear later, independently. We do not know whether these

47

fugitive pieces were collected and published by their authors;
if so, one imagines them to have been *éditions de luxe*, such as
Lygdamus' *Neaera*.[1] The lesser poets around Messalla wrote in
a similar vein. Their social background and style of living is
certainly the same.

One example may be sufficient to show the kind of erotic
poetry that was written around 100 B.C. by these noble dilettanti.
The pretty lines of Q. Lutatius Catulus (consul 102 B.C.):

> *Aufugit mi animus; credo, ut solet, ad Theotimum*
>   *devenit. Sic est; perfugium illud habet.*
> *Quid, si non interdixem, ne illunc fugitivum*
>   *mitteret ad se intro, sed magis eiceret?*
> *Ibimus quaesitum. Verum, ne ipsi teneamur*
>   *formido. Quid ago? Da, Venus, consilium.*
>
> (Gellius, *Noct. Att.* 19.9.14)

are modelled after an epigram by Callimachus (41, Pf.). The concept that the soul (or half of the soul) of the lover escapes, in a
kiss or by the sheer force of desire, appears in many variations
in the Greek love-poems of Meleager's *Garland*.[2]

Catulus has not produced a straight translation of the Greek
original which must have been famous. He has kept the same
number of lines, and the sequence of thought in the first two
distichs corresponds to that of Callimachus. But he has simplified
Callimachus' concept of the divided soul; *his* soul has left him
altogether. Moreover, he has replaced the Greek poet's vague
indication 'to some youth' by a concrete name, Theotimus.[3]
Finally, he has modified the last distich considerably. Callimachus
contents himself with a sigh of resignation; the Roman poet goes

---

[1] *Corp. Tibull.* 3.1.9-14.

[2] First in Plato, *Anth. Pal.* 5.78, it seems. The theme appealed to all the major
poets of Meleager's *Garland* in turn: Asclepiades, *Anth. Pal.* 12.166; Callimachus;
Meleager himself, *Anth. Pal.* 5.171. On its use in later literature see S. Gaselee in
The Criterion (1924), 349ff; on its philosophical interpretation A. J. Festugière,
Rev. Études Grecques (1952), 260; A. D. Nock, *Gnomon* (1957), 526.

[3] Unless, in Callimachus' epigram, the name is hidden at the beginning of v. 5
where the MS. reading is obviously corrupt (cf. E. Schwyzer, *Rh. Mus.* 1928, 261;
F. Dornseiff, *Symb. Osl.* 1953, 27ff). If Callimachus really did omit the name, the
difference from his Roman imitator is more striking. The Hellenistic poet is in love
but with no definite person in mind; his is not a love 'for somebody' (Plato, *Banquet*,
p. 199D).

through several moods – resignation, firm decision, hesitation and admission of defeat.

Catulus and his fellow poets are well-read in Greek poetry. They know Sappho, Callimachus and Meleager; but their taste is Alexandrian and they rely on literary technique and mannerisms. On the whole their poems are rather impersonal. They record delicate feelings and offer elaborate compliments, not without grace but a little stiffly, as if they were to be engraved on a diploma.

All of them must have patronized Greek men of letters and one of them – probably the poet Archias – may have introduced them to Meleager's *Garland*.¹ But none of them seems to have translated or slavishly imitated a Greek original. There is always a new touch, and sometimes the motifs of two or more Hellenistic epigrams are combined. There is a feeling of competition with the Greeks. These Roman writers stayed just close enough to their models for any educated reader to be able to recognize the allusion; in fact, they invited such comparisons in order to prove that they had gone, in one or two points, beyond the original.

Such *poésies d'occasion* know little or nothing of the tensions and the tragic disquietude revealed in the best work of Catullus or Propertius. In spite of their technical competence they remain anonymous, so to speak, because none of them grows out of a deep personal experience.

Both Propertius and Ovid have listed the names of erotic poets whom they may very well have considered as their predecessors. In an elegy which was written between 29 and 26 B.C., Propertius (2.34B) defends his own love-poetry and love-poetry in general. Even Vergil, the poet of the *Aeneid*, has once, in a playful mood, sung of the love of shepherds (67–76). With a rapid transition whose meaning we can only guess (the text is doubtful, 83f), he adds the names of four other erotic poets, Varro of Atax, Catullus, Calvus, Gallus and himself, devoting a distich to each. These distichs follow the same pattern; they include the name of the poet's mistress (to whom, we must assume, his work was dedicated), and each hexameter ends on the name of the poet

---

¹ This is the hypothesis of J. Hubaux, *Les Thèmes bucoliques dans la poésie latine* (1930), 26ff. Archias was personally acquainted with Catulus; his own epigrams show that he had read Meleager's *Garland*.

himself. Such a parallelism suggests that Propertius may have left out other names, simply because they did not fit into his pattern.

Indeed, the list we find in Ovid's *Tristia* 2.427ff (written in A.D. 9) is considerably longer. Besides those names mentioned by Propertius, he has ten others: Ticidas, Memmius, Cinna, Anser, Cornificius, Valerius Cato, Hortensius, Servius, Sisenna and Tibullus (and, of course, himself). His list must be fairly complete since he is interested in including every name that could possibly be included, in order to show that the publication of love-poetry never was and never should be a criminal offence in Rome. He has, however, omitted certain names, notably that of Laevius, the author of *Erotopaignia*; but also Cornelius Nepos and Q. Mucius Scaevola, whose erotic verse the younger Pliny read (*Epist.* 5.3.5 and 6); and there may have been still others of whom we do not know.

On the whole, Propertius' list seems more representative. Some of the authors included in Ovid's catalogue have little significance for the history of the Latin love-elegy. We can eliminate the dilettanti such as Memmius, the political adventurer to whom Lucretius had dedicated his poem on Nature, Cornificius (one of Caesar's officers, governor of Cilicia, 46 B.C.), Hortensius, the orator, and Servius Sulpicius Rufus, the jurist. We can further eliminate Ticidas (not a pseudonym; he has been identified with one of Caesar's officers), Cinna, Anser and Sisenna, either because they did not write in the elegiac metre or because too little is known about them. What is left is substantially Propertius' list, with the addition of Valerius Cato. These are the authors that must be dealt with in the history of the Latin erotic elegy, but we shall never know what their significance was, since practically all they wrote is lost.[1]

Calvus recorded his 'erotic adventures' (*furta*) in various metres (Ovid, *loc. cit.*). He is also remembered for his elegy (or elegies?) on the death of his wife Quintilia. Nothing is known of

[1] It is probable that most of them belonged to the same literary group; they were the *poetae novi*, the 'modern poets' (ridiculed by Cicero as *Cantores Euphorionis*, *Tusc. Disp.* 3.45). We know that they were roughly contemporaries and that some of them were personal friends of Catullus. There was a lady among them, who was celebrated in the poems of her friends under a pseudonym, Perilla, and wrote verse under her real name. Metella.

this funeral poem beyond two short fragments. Still, it is easy to speculate on its form and content. As one of the leaders of the school of the 'modern poets', Calvus probably knew Antimachus' *Lyde* and Parthenius' elegy on the death of his wife Arete. Whether he was able to avoid their influence altogether is doubtful. In any event, his was a strong personal experience; after the playful experiment of Catulus and others, the record of a deeply felt emotion was something new.

Valerius Cato wrote, perhaps, the *Lydia*, a curious mixture of bucolic and erotic poetry. He was a very learned author, a man of sharp critical taste and, like Calvus, one of Catullus' close friends. Two other works of his are mentioned, *Diana* (an epyllion or an aetiological poem?) and *Indignatio*, an autobiographical poem. Ovid calls Valerius Cato's love-poems 'frivolous' and compares them to the verse of Cornificius. Propertius omits his name, perhaps because none of his works dealt with personal experience or because no woman played in it the role of Lesbia or Cynthia.

The most controversial figure in the history of the Latin erotic elegy is Cornelius Gallus. His life is fairly well known.[1] We can follow his brilliant rise to success and fame and his sudden fall. We can understand that he fascinated his own generation and that his memory stayed alive for a long time. But we know very little about the character of his poetry.

He was born in 70/69 B.C. at Forum Iuli (Fréjus) in Gallia Narbonensis. His distinguished career as an officer and administrator led to his appointment as the first prefect of Egypt, Augustus' personal province. He now became over-confident, assumed credit for some of Augustus' achievements, was denounced to the Emperor, and fell in disgrace. In 26 B.C. he died by his own hand.

Between his campaigns he had found time to compose four books of love-elegies (and other works). These four books were probably published under the title *Amores*, with the subtitle *Lycoris*, the name which he gave to his mistress Cytheris, a Greek freedwoman. Her legal name, after the *manumissio*, was Volumnia. When he met her, she had already been the mistress of two public figures, M. Iunius Brutus and M. Antonius, the triumvir. Soon enough she exchanged Gallus for another lover.

[1] Cf. R. Syme, *Class. Quart.* (1938), 39ff.

It was this experience that may have made a poet of Gallus. Many years later, Martial writes: *Ingenium Galli pulchra Lycoris erat* (8.73.6), 'beautiful Lycoris was Gallus' genius'. She was to him what Cynthia was to Propertius: *ingenium nobis ipsa puella facit* (Propertius 2.1.4), 'the girl herself is the cause of our genius'. Gallus may have written verse before and after his association with Cytheris – but the one work which established his reputation was his collection of love-elegies.

'The love of Gallus' is the theme of Vergil's tenth Eclogue. Gallus, deserted by Lycoris, nurses his grief, and all nature and the gods are sympathizing with him. He replies with a song – a song in praise of the bucolic landscape in which he hoped to live with Lycoris. He sings of the cool springs, the soft meadows, and the grove where they might have spent happy years together. For a moment it seems as though he might find comfort in a bucolic life; he even announces that he will recast the verse he once composed in the manner of Euphorion into bucolic rhythms. He realizes that there is no remedy for his love:

> 'Love conquers all things; yield we too to love.'

According to one of the ancient commentaries on Vergil's *Eclogues* (Servius on v. 46), this love song is substantially derived from Gallus' own poems. The wording of Servius' note is a little vague: *hi . . . omnes versus Galli sunt de ipsius translati carminibus*, 'all these lines of Gallus are derived from his own poems'. This means that Vergil has taken a few characteristic themes from Gallus' collection of elegies and 'recast them into bucolic rhythms'; he has done himself, in other words, what Gallus merely planned to do, as if he wanted to set an example. It does not follow from Servius' note that the bucolic mood of the whole passage is characteristic of Gallus' elegies.

Only one line survives from Gallus' *Amores*; it tells us very little about the content and character of this work. Quintilian (*Inst. Or.* 10.1.93) calls him *durior*, 'rather harsh', but whether this criticism refers to Gallus' style or metre we do not know.

We know, however, that mythology played a considerable role in his elegies. Parthenius of Nicae dedicated a collection of love-stories to him hoping that he might 'draw from it material, as may seem suitable to you for epic and elegiac poems' (Preface).[1] Does this mean that Gallus used this material for purely mythological elegies in the manner of the Alexandrian poets, dedicating the whole collection to Lycoris? Or was the book really about his love to Lycoris, with mythological examples serving as illustrations in the manner of Propertius?

Parthenius seems to have left the decision to Gallus. If the Roman poet followed the example of his Greek friend, he probably wrote in the Alexandrian manner. There is evidence that his interests tended in this direction. Another of Vergil's commentators, Probus (on *Ecl.* 10.50), notes that (*Euphorionis*) *in scribendo secutus colorem videtur Cornelius Gallus*, 'Cornelius Gallus seems to have followed in writing the manner of Euphorion'. Again we do not know whether this note refers to love-elegies or to one of Gallus' mythological poems, 'the Grove of Grynium', a translation from Euphorion.

When Gallus planned (or published) this poem, Vergil congratulated him on his endeavour. In the sixth Eclogue Silenus deals with many themes in his song[2]; one of them is Gallus' consecration as a poet. Gallus, he relates, was wandering by the Permessus, when he encountered one of the Muses. She led him up to the Aonian mountains where the other Muses and Apollo himself rose to greet him (Vergil, *Ecl.* 6.64ff). Linus, the legendary singer, offers him on behalf of the Muses the reeds that were once given to Hesiod, in order that Gallus may record the 'birth of the Grynean grove'.

The meaning of this allegory is clear enough. Without stressing the geographical details one may say this: by translating (or adapting) Euphorion's work, Gallus becomes at the same time a successor of Hesiod, the master of mythological (non-epic) poetry. What has he been before? He was a wanderer in the valley of the Permessus, that is, a love-poet. Propertius, in a similar situation, hesitating between love-poetry and poetry 'in the manner of Hesiod', admits that so far his poems have only been dipped by Amor into Permessus' stream and do not yet know the 'sources of Hesiod', that is to say, the water from

---

[1] On the preface of Parthenius' 'Love-Romances' see E. Rohde, *Der griech. Roman* (third ed. 1916), 121, and F. Zimmermann's commentary, *Hermes* (1934), 179ff.

[2] Cf. G. Luck, *Gnomon* (1955), 606.

which Hesiod drank (Propertius 2.10.25f).[1] Needless to say, this Vergilian passage tells us nothing about the *character* of Gallus' love-poems.

These are the scanty facts. They have been combined by the scholars to support various speculations. For a long time it has been customary to hail Gallus as the founder of the 'subjective' erotic elegy in Rome. But all we really know from the testimonies is the fact that he was at one time in love with Lycoris, that she treated him cruelly, that he wrote poems about or to her, and that she became known through these poems:

> *Gallus et Hesperiis et Gallus notus Eois,*
> *et sua cum Gallo nota Lycoris erit.*

'Gallus shall be known to the inhabitants of the West and to those of the East, and known with Gallus shall be his Lycoris.'
(Ovid, Amores 1.15.29f)

Propertius in the catalogue of love-poets (2.34.87f and 93f) introduces both Catullus and himself in a similar manner: he says that Lesbia became better known than Helena through Catullus' poems and that his own elegies were written 'in praise of Cynthia'.

This still does not mean that Gallus wrote about his own experience or about typical ones that might have been his own. Lycoris' fame is solid enough if she just inspired the poet to write – mythological poems, epyllia or anything else. She was still his *ingenium*; she still made him what he was. But he must have said so in his book. On the other hand, both Ovid (*Tristia* 4.10.51-4) and Quintilian (*Inst. Or.* 10.1.93) consider him as part of the group of elegiac poets.

Varro of Atax, one of the *poetae novi*, was remembered as the author of *Argonautica*. When he had finished this work he composed love-poems[2] – unlike Vergil or Ovid, who wrote love-poetry in their youth and did not attempt to compose an epic until later in life.

Varro's mistress was introduced under the name Leucadia, a name that fits as well into a hexameter (or pentameter) as Lesbia.

---

[1] Cf. p. 135f; J. P. Elder, *Harv. Stud. Class. Philol.* 65 (1961), 110.

[2] Propertius 2.34.85, *haec quoque* (= 'love-poetry such as yours') *perfecto ludebat Iasone Varro*; Ovid, *Tristia* 2.439f, *is quoque Phasiacas Argon qui duxit in undas, non potuit Veneris furta tacere suae.*

It may have been chosen for the same reason. The reader should remember Sappho, the 'Tenth Muse' (cf. Propertius 2.30.37ff).[1] Like Cynthia, like Sulpicia, like Ovid's friend Perilla (*Trist.* 3.7), these ladies knew and appreciated Greek and Latin poetry, and they may have written verse themselves in either language. It was not enough merely to be beautiful.

Propertius' testimony is unusual because he refers to *Leucadiae maxima flamma suae*, 'the extraordinary passion of his (Varro's) beloved Leucadia'. This should indicate mutual love, a happy relationship, especially if it is contrasted with Propertius' statement on Gallus and Lycoris.

That Varro wrote about his own erotic adventures is suggested by Ovid, *Tristia* 2.439f, *non potuit Veneris furta tacere suae*, 'he could not keep silent about his own erotic adventures'. Those 'secret adventures' do not necessarily mean that his love for Leucadia (or any other woman) was adulterous. They merely indicate 'romantic adventures' or 'secret affairs'. Neither Ovid not Propertius tells us anything about the character of Varro's erotic poetry.

Some other names are mentioned occasionally, for instance, C. Valgius Rufus, elegiac poet and scholar, and one of Horace's intimate friends, a man on whose judgement he depended. Like Horace, he was a member of Maecenas' circle. He may have had connexions with Messalla's circle as well, for the anonymous author of the *Panegyricus Messallae* (V. 180) places Valgius on the same level as Homer.[2]

Horace addressed one of his most beautiful odes to Valgius (Horace c. 2.9), urging him to cease the laments over the death of the handsome boy Mystes and to celebrate Augustus' victories instead. He calls these laments *flebiles modi*, perhaps because they were in the elegiac metre. The theme – love of a handsome boy – reminds one of Phanocles' *Erotes* or Tibullus' group of Marathus-poems. Parthenius and Calvus also wrote elegies on the death of someone they loved. There may have been reminiscences of all of them in Valgius' verse. Since Horace calls him back to the

---

[1] Sappho is the first woman to be called a 'mortal Muse' (by Antipater of Sidon, *Anth. Pal.* 7.14).

[2] His name has even been slipped into Tibullus' earliest elegy, 1.10, by textual conjecture (v. 11); but this is doubtful, see Gundel, RE 8A.272f.

present in such forceful terms, it is probable that Valgius sought comfort in the legends of the past, as Antimachus seems to have done before him in a similar situation.

Of all the many 'unknown poets' of the first century B.C. we shall mention only one more, Domitius Marsus, whose moving lines on Tibullus' death allude to one of Tibullus' earlier elegies (1.3.58, also imitated by Ovid in his elegy on Tibullus' death, *Amores* 3.9.60).

There is no evidence that Marsus wrote elegies, but Martial (2.77.5f) speaks about his epigrams, and we know the name of a girl, *fusca Melaenis*, 'dark Melaenis' who seems to have played a certain role in his life and verse. Melaenis is a 'speaking' name, such as those of artisans or fishermen in Books VI and VII of the Greek Anthology; and lovely dark girls are often praised in the erotic epigrams of Book V. The title *Cicuta*, of one of Marsus' published volumes, is known and seems to have dealt at least partly with contemporary literary figures.[1]

Catullus is the first Latin love-poet whose works are extant. He is the first Latin poet whose work is dominated by a great passion, the first who has created verse in which this passion lives on for ever. Cornelius Gallus is little more than a name for us. We know too little about his contributions to the themes and the character of elegiac poetry as a whole, and hence we must consider Catullus as the first representative of the erotic elegy in its Roman form.

To show his influence we might collect the passages in the later elegists which reflect thoughts or images of Catullus. There are a great many, but a list of them, if it could ever be complete, would prove nothing. It is enough to say that Propertius, Tibullus and Ovid, as well as the minor talents of Messalla's circle, were thoroughly familiar with Catullus' poetry.

It is misleading, however, to speak of 'imitations of Catullus'. He himself 'imitated' the Alexandrian poets; and passages in later elegists reminding us of him may be inspired directly by the Alexandrians (Callimachus above all) whom Catullus recognized

[1] Two epigrams of Domitius Marsus were recently found in an anthology of Latin poetry compiled around A.D. 400, the so-called *Epigrammata Bobiensia*. Both deal with Octavius' mother, Atia; the first (nr. 40) claims to be her epitaph. Both were probably included in the *Cicuta*.

as his masters. The search for 'parallels' is only meaningful if the variations of each 'parallel' are interpreted as an expression of the poet's individuality.

Catullus is recognized by Propertius and Ovid as one of the representatives of the elegiac tradition. Tibullus, who never mentions any other poets, living or dead, pays an occasional compliment to Catullus by varying one of his themes. Lygdamus (*Corp. Tibull.* 3.6.41) quotes the 'polished Catullus', *doctus Catullus*, once, as if to acknowledge a debt which is, indeed, obvious.

Propertius calls him *lascivus* and declares that Lesbia is better known than Helen of Troy, thanks to his writings (Propertius 2.34.87f). Ovid (*Tristia* 2.427ff) repeats the epithet *lascivus* and adds that Catullus also 'revealed' many other love-affairs, admitting his 'intrigues', *adulterium*.[1] In his funeral elegy on Tibullus, he has a vision of Catullus and Calvus in the underworld coming to meet Tibullus:

> *Obvius huic venias hedera iuvenalia cinctus*
> *tempora cum Calvo, docte Catulle, tuo.*
> (Ovid, Amores 3.9.61f)

But since he did not publish a full book of elegies, he is sometimes excluded from the 'canon' of the elegists, as, for example, in Quintilian's survey of Latin literature (*Inst. Or.* 10.1.93).

It is difficult to imagine in what direction the Latin love-elegy would have developed without Catullus. The very fact that he lived and wrote at a particular time, under particular circumstances – the very fact that he was the kind of man, the kind of poet he was, is simple enough to grasp, genius is always unique. Even from a purely technical point of view his influence cannot be underestimated. He admired and adapted Callimachus and the other Alexandrians, and henceforth these standards were accepted by the elegiac poets.

The ancient literary critics distinguished sharply between lyric and elegiac poetry. For Catullus as well as for the Greeks, metre was not an accidental matter, a kind of exterior ornament which may or may not be chosen. It was intimately connected with the

---

[1] This may refer to Catullus' c. 111 (see Ellis' note).

theme and mood of the poem as a whole. When Catullus chose the elegiac distich rather than the hexameter or the hendecasyllable for a particular poem, he did so because he thought he needed the musical appeal of the pentameter to enhance his feeling.

We have three long elegies of Catullus (cc. 66, 67 and 68). Each of them represents a different type of elegiac poem, and none of them is an erotic elegy in the manner of Propertius, Tibullus or Ovid. The 'Lock of Berenice' (c. 66) is a learned mythological poem without connexion to Catullus' own experience, only indirectly concerned with love, and, above all, a more or less free adaptation from the Greek.

Catullus' c. 67 is a blend of the *paraclausithyron*[1] (the 'serenade of the shut-out lover') and a satire, with a predominance of the satirical mood. The situation may be concrete enough and the reference to living persons quite unmistakable to any contemporary reader; but it is no love-poem in the ordinary sense of the word.

His third long elegy, c. 68, is even more complex; it is a poetic epistle, a mythological poem, a love-elegy and a dirge at the same time. It is possible that Catullus found in Alexandrian literature certain prototypes for such an extravagant blend of different poetic *genera*. It is even more likely that Catullus, a creative poet in his own right, and always anxious to experiment, has made the elegiac distich a vehicle of very heterogeneous thoughts and emotions, in a long and consciously artful poem.[2]

From many points of view, it represents the prototype of the Latin erotic elegy. It is also one of the most beautiful poems ever written in Latin. I should like to give a full translation of it – knowing that this is an almost impossible task.[3] Many translators

---

[1] There is now a useful study of the 'serenade of the shut-out lover', F. O. Copley, *Exclusus Amator. A Study in Latin Love Poetry*, 1955 (Monogr. Am. Philol. Ass., 17), but I disagree with Mr Copley on a few points; see my review in *Gnomon* 29 (1957), pp. 338ff.

[2] On the 'mixture of literary *genera*' as a characteristic of Latin literature in general see W. Kroll, *Studien zum Verständnis der römischen Literatur* (1926), 202-224. It was R. Heinze's thesis that the existence of the more complex art form proves the previous existence of more simple forms.

[3] The translations from Catullus in Gilbert Highet's *Poets in a Landscape* (Alfred Knopf, New York, 1957) are excellent. I list the fragments from our poem in the

have given us a Catullus who is frozen in unbearably noble postures, lyre in hand, his eyes turned toward heaven. Others, no less regrettably, have presented us a Catullus in bedroom slippers, a cigarette dangling from his mouth. It is one of the characteristics of Catullus' style that he blends the grand manner with deliberate colloquialisms, in one and the same poem. It would be entirely wrong to select a certain tone or rhythm beforehand – that of Swinburne, for example – and pour Catullus' verse into this new mould. Unless the translator is a very gifted poet himself, he is bound to fail. The real challenge consists in staying as closely as possible to the original, without violating the usages of the modern idiom.

CATULLUS TO ALLIUS

Overwhelmed by bitter misfortune, you send me
  this little letter, written with your tears,
and expect me to lift up and bring back from the threshold of death
  the shipwrecked cast out by the foaming waves of the sea
whom Venus, the goddess, lets not enjoy soft sleep   5
  as he rests deserted and lonely in his bed;
nor do the Muses of ancient poets comfort him with song,
  as his tortured mind finds no sleep.
It makes me happy that you call me your friend
  and ask me for the gifts of the Muses and Venus: 10

---

order of lines: 15-24 (Highet, p. 7), 27-36 (p. 41), 57-61 (p. 17), 66-72 (p. 17), 135-140 (p. 19). I realize the shortcomings of my renderings when I compare it with Mr Highet's elegant and accomplished version. On one point, I have to disagree with him (and other scholars). It concerns the lines 27ff.

> *Quare, quod scribis Veronae turpe Catullo*
> *Esse, quod hic quisquis de meliore nota*
> *Frigida deserto tepefactet membra cubili,*
> *Id, Mani, non est turpe, magis miserumst.*

Mr Highet (following Vahlen) understands the 'bed' in line 29 as Lesbia's bed in Rome, in which the social élite, during Catullus' absence, are warming their cold limbs. But *hic* (v. 28) seems to refer to Verona where Catullus stays; it corresponds to the locative *Veronae*. I cannot believe that this should be taken as a quotation from Allius' letter (*hic* = *Romae*). Catullus wants to say that it is impossible for him to have a love-affair in the small city where everything that the élite does becomes immediately the subject of gossip. *Tepefactet* is also significant; it means 'tries to keep warm' which is difficult because he has to sleep 'alone' – this is the meaning of *desertum* (cf. v. 6). If Catullus were referring to Rome, he would use not *hic*, but *istic* (as Ovid always does, in his letters from exile).

but, Manius, you must know of my own troubles
   lest you think that I hate the duties of friendship;
when you know in what floods of misery I am drowned,
   you will no longer ask a poor man for substantial gifts.

At the time when I first was given the white toga,   15
   when the wonderful spring of my life was in bloom,
I played the game of love a good deal. The goddess
   who blends sweet bitterness with cares knows me well.
But the grief at my brother's death took away all inclination.
   (Alas, dear brother! taken away from me,   20
you shattered my happiness when you died, dear brother,
   and our whole house was buried with you.
All my pleasures perished with you, my pleasures
   which your sweet affection nourished while you lived.)
When he died, I dismissed from my soul altogether   25
   the temptations and all the pleasures of my heart.

And now you write that it is a shame for Catullus
   to be in Verona where everybody who is anybody
tries to warm his cold limbs in an empty bed:
   that, Manius, is not a shame; it is a pity.   30
You will forgive me if I cannot offer you
   the tokens of friendship which my grief took away.
I do not have with me many books;
   because I live in Rome, my house is there,
my home is there, and there I spend my life.   35
   Only one book-box from many has travelled with me.
Under these circumstances, do not think me selfish
   to act like this, or not generous enough.
Because the double grant, which you request and I refuse
   I would offer gladly if it were not denied me.   40

I must tell you, Muses, of the help that Allius gave to me
   and in how many ways he helped me,
lest the flight of time and the oblivion of centuries
   cover that devotion of his with impenetrable night.
Yes, I shall tell you, and you in turn, tell it to many thousands;   45
   let this page of mine be eloquent in the distant future . . .
. . .
   and after his death let him be known more and more,

nor let the spider weaving in the air its web
   cover the abandoned name of Allius. 50

You know the deceitful cares which the goddess of love once gave me,
   and in what ways she brought about my downfall,
when I was burning inside as mount Aetna,
   and the hot springs of Malis near Thermopylae on Oeta;
when the lustre of my eyes was dimmed by incessant tears 55
   and my cheeks always wet with the rain of sadness,
as a stream bursts forth, shining on the top of a mountain, high up
      in the air;
   from the moss-covered rocks
it rushes downward through the steep valley,
   and crosses a highway where many travellers pass — 60
a sweet refreshment to the weary perspiring wanderer,
   when heavy heat splits the parched fields.

In this predicament, Allius' help was to me
   what a favouring breeze, blowing so gently,
means to the sailors tossed about in a black whirlpool, 65
   after they have addressed already their prayers to Pollux and Castor.
He opened up wide to me a field closed before
   and gave to me and my lady his house
where we could meet and fulfil our mutual love —
   the house which my lady entered, gracefully moving — a luminous
      goddess! — 70
and touched with her shining soles
   in clicking sandals the worn-out threshold.

Thus, ardent with love for her husband, came
   Laodamia to Protesilaus' house,
a house built in vain; no sacrificial victim had pacified 75
   with its blood the heavenly gods.
(O Nemesis, goddess of Rhamnus, may nothing ever entice me so
      strongly
   that I would frivolously grasp it against the will of the gods!)
When Laodamia had lost her husband, she knew at once
   how much the altar, left thirsting, had desired the blood of a
      holy offering. 80

She was forced to let go from her embrace her young husband
   before the long nights of a winter or two, perhaps,
had satisfied her avid desire
   and helped her to live when their marriage was shattered.
The Fates knew: it would not last long,   85
   if he departed as a warrior for the walls of Troy.

Troy had brought up at the time in arms against herself,
   by the abduction of Helen, the princes of the Argives,
Troy (what a crime!), the common tomb of Asia and Europe;
   Troy, the bitter end of so many brave men.   90
(Did she not bring a lamentable death to my brother, too?
   Alas, dear brother! taken away from me,
alas! cherished apple of my eye, taken away from your brother!
   Our whole house was buried with you,
and all my pleasures perished with you,   95
   the pleasures which your sweet affection nourished while you lived.
But a foreign ground holds you, far away, at the end of the world,
   buried near Troy the repulsive, Troy the unlucky city;
you have not been laid to rest among the tombs you knew,
   not near the burial place of our family.)   100

The story goes that the young men from all of Greece
   had left their homes and hearths to hurry to Troy,
lest Paris, who had abducted triumphantly the adulterous woman
   might enjoy undisturbed leisure in his bedroom.
Such a disaster, lovely Laodamia, bereft you of your husband   105
   who was sweeter to you than your life and soul.
Your passionate love engulfed you in such a whirlpool
   and suddenly dragged you down to its bottom,
as the whirlpool near Cyllene in Pheneos, described by the Greeks,
   which dries the rich soil by sucking in its moisture –   110
(the glory of having dug it by carving through the mountain,
   belongs to Heracles, wrongly known as Amphitryo's son,
at the time when he pierced with unfailing arrows the monstrous
           Stymphalian birds,
   obeying the order of that king who was a lesser hero than he,
so that the door of heaven should be crowded by one more god,   115
   and Hebe not stay an unwed virgin forever)

62

— yes, your deep love was deeper than that whirlpool,
  your love which made you bear the yoke of wedlock, untamed
      before.

The only daughter of a man wasting away with age,
  never gave such happiness to her father by bringing up a late-
      born son   120
whose name is written into the will, confirmed by witnesses;
  he is greeted at last as the heir of his grandfather's wealth;
he destroys the ruthless hopes of the next-of-kin, and makes him a
      laughing-stock,
  chasing the vulture from his grandfather's grey head.
Never has any dove rejoiced so much in the love of her shining
      companion —   125
  (and doves are said to pluck their kisses with less inhibition,
using their beaks to bite,
  than a woman whose desires are omnivorous) —
but your love alone surpassed these great examples,
  once you were given in marriage to your fair-haired groom.   130

My love rushed into my embrace as beautiful and passionate
  — or hardly less so — as Laodamia,
and Cupid, shining in his purple garment
  flew in circles around and about her.
And if she is not satisfied with Catullus alone,   135
  I shall bear the occasional infidelities of my lady who is faithful
      in her fashion,
lest I annoy her foolishly with my jealousies.
  Juno, the greatest among the heavenly goddesses
often digested her wrath at her husband's guilty passions,
  when she found out about the countless infidelities of insatiable
      Jove.   140
Yet neither is it fair to compare men to gods . . .
. . .
  (?) Relieve your tremulous father of his heavy burden (?)
And yet she did not come to me, led by her father's hand,   145
  to a house perfumed with Assyrian fragrances,
but now and then, at night, she gave me secret tokens of her love,
  stolen boldly from her husband's embrace.

It is enough if she gives to me alone that happy day
  which she marks in my calendar with white chalk.   150

This gift – it is all I have – consisting of a poem,
  is dispatched to you, Allius, for the sake of the many proofs of
      your friendship,
lest the rust of decay infect your name,
  in the course of time and ever more time to come.
To this the gods may add most of the gifts which Themis   155
  bestowed once on the righteous men of a distant Golden Age.

Be happy, you and your love, and the house
  where I and my lady have played the game of love – may it be
      happy, too,
and he who put firm ground under me, in the beginning . . . (?)
  who was the origin of all my happiness,   160
and she who is dearer to me than anyone else, dearer to me than
      myself,
  my love, who brightens my life as long as she lives.

This elegy may be an experiment, but the fact remains that it
deals with the poet's own experience. Is it, then, a subjective
elegy with mythological digressions? The legends which Catullus
conjures up (Troy, the love of Laodamia) become the background
of intense moments in his own life (his worship of Lesbia, his
brother's death). He needs these myths not only because they
enable him to show his skill in bringing out the pictorial or
sentimental values of his theme, but also because the language
of mythology represents the deepest realities in a sort of shorthand.

The individual themes of this elegy succeed each other in an
order that reveals the poet's conscious care. He relies on contrast
and correspondence to create surprising new effects. His friendship for Allius, the loss of his brother, his devotion to Lesbia – in
short, the delights and disenchantments of his life acquire a new
meaning, reflected in the magic mirror of the legendary past.

It would be possible to dissect the poem in its elements and to
trace their history through Latin elegiac poetry. But what really
matters is the fact that they all occur in the same poem, that they

take up approximately the same number of lines,[1] and that they are interwoven in the most intricate manner. The whole procedure is so singular that we should look, perhaps, for an explanation that is psychological rather than purely literary.[2]

The pattern of c. 68 never became popular among Catullus' successors, no doubt because the technical difficulty discouraged them. Another reason, far more important, I believe, lies in the fact that the emotional situation of Catullus at that time could not be stripped off like a glove to fit someone else's individuality.

Catullus' situation is by no means typical. Not his own personal love-experience, but that of his friend Allius forms the theme of the introductory lines. Allius, not Catullus, is caught in a predicament which the later elegists might recognize as typical. The transition which enables Catullus to introduce his own love as a parallel theme is singularly flat and prosaic:

> sed tibi ne mea sint ignota incommoda, Mani, . . .
>
> (v. 11)

Now the poem seems to turn into a love-elegy, but after a brief mention of the erotic adventures of his adolescent years, Catullus dwells on his brother's death, and we realize that his 'sufferings', incommoda, have a much larger meaning, beyond everything Allius had to endure.

Allius is, indeed, the conventional lover; he writes his letter to Catullus 'in tears'; he feels close to death; he waits in his lonely bed in vain for sleep to come; he finds no comfort in poetry. Every single one of these themes is echoed many times in Propertius, Tibullus and Ovid.[3] But this is precisely the part of Catullus' poem which is not concerned with himself. As soon as he turns to his own situation, he finds an idiom all his own,

---

[1] The lament for his dead brother takes up only ten lines, but in the very centre of the poem (vv. 91-100), after being referred to in the introduction (vv. 19-26). The landscape of Troy serves as a transition. It is dealt with in $(4+4=8$ lines). Catullus' love for Lesbia $(22+10=32$ lines) and the friendship with Allius $(6+4$ lines in the introduction and $10+8$ lines in the main poem, $=28$ lines) and the myth of Protesilaus and Laodamia $(14+16=30$ lines) take up approximately the same space.

[2] This approach has been suggested by J. P. Elder, Harv. Stud. Class. Phil. (1951), 101ff.

[3] Allius' letter 'written in tears', cf. Propertius 4.3.3f, Ovid, Heroides 3.3; Allius close to death, cf. Propertius 1.19, etc.; Allius sleepless in his lonely bed, cf. Ovid, Amores 1.2; Allius unable to find comfort in poetry, cf. Tibullus 2.4.13, etc.

difficult to recapture. Hardly any parallels to this part can be found in later poets.

It might be argued that it was Catullus' treatment of the myth rather than any individual thought or turn of the phrase that became fruitful for the later development of the Roman elegy. But again, Catullus' effort to transform his experience into the marvellous and mythical is not really a 'device' that can be applied independently of its own context. It has a freshness and originality all its own. The revelation of Lesbia's beauty as she steps over the threshold (vv. 70ff) is a vision deeply seen and felt and strikingly expressed.

The main themes as well as the structure of Catullus c. 68 reflect the poet's situation. It is so complex that it does not fit into any traditional literary form. He sees the present as a result of the past (his own past), but both present and past blend into one before the background of the myth. Hence, the myth, far from being an external decoration, establishes the unity of the poem; it concentrates many years into one intense moment.

Since Catullus c. 68 is such a personal kind of poem, it seems unwise to stress its role within the development of the Latin love-elegy.[1] There is a group of short erotic poems in the elegiac metre, Catullus' 'epigrams', for example, cc. 72, 73, 75, 76, 83, 85, 87, 92, 107, 109. They are all personal documents, not merely literary exercises, and they all deal with Catullus' love for Lesbia. Their very conciseness represents a challenge requiring a clear thought, a precise phrase, a polished image. Catullus himself calls these poems *nugae*, 'nothings', but they are the product of *doctus labor*, 'conscious literary technique', and he expects them to live 'for more than a century'. In other words, he felt confident that they would stand comparison with Philetas' παίγνια and Meleager's 'Flowers'.

If Catullus preferred the short elegiac poem for his most intimate confessions (c. 85), he must have had a definite artistic purpose in mind. It was not that he felt unable to compose a long elegy in the manner that became accepted among his successors; he simply said what he had to say and left it at that. Regardless of how much he may have polished them, they sound true, and

[1] Butler and Barber, *The Elegies of Propertius* (1933), lix, reach the same conclusion after a careful discussion of the facts.

their tone is unmistakably Catullus' own. Again, his successors were faced with a serious disadvantage. What Catullus had done, could not be done all over again. The poetry of Propertius, for instance, represents just as much a reaction against Catullus as it shows his concrete influence.

It is pointless to argue whether c. 76

Siqua recordanti benefacta priora voluptas . . .

is an elegy or an epigram. It is a love-poem, one of the most beautiful of Catullus' love-poems; at the same time it is an *adhortatio ad se ipsum*. Like cc. 85, 72 and 75, it portrays the poet's struggle between love and hate, but it is written in a more contemplative mood. For one moment Catullus sees a way out of his conflict. He has found the strength to pray to the gods. His personal experience becomes part of a universal experience, and his love appears not merely as an irrational drive, but as a selfless act, a gift that was offered and refused.

It would be misleading to call this poem a mere elaboration of epigrammatic themes. It has obviously been conceived and planned as an elegy. The calm and graceful progression of its main thought, the rhythms and the parallel clauses, its full and rounded expression – all this is art that works with a minimum of effects, worthy of the best classical manner. It is doubtful whether any Alexandrian poet ever wrote (or could have written!) lines such as these.

The religious mood of the poem, too, goes beyond the mood or fancy of the moment. Catullus knows that the gods will reward his *pietas* (v. 26), the *sancta fides* (v. 3) which he had observed all his life. His passion was a 'disease' (*pestis, pernicies, taeter morbus*), but now that he has found the way out of the dark labyrinth into an ordered and meaningful world, in which a pure conduct of life is valued, he sees his whole life in a new light.

And all this rings true; we feel that Catullus has broken through the conventions of love-poetry where life is necessarily over-shadowed by the great passion, ruled by the arbitrary law of Venus and Cupid. Both Tibullus and Propertius also feel the need of relating their individual experience to some higher, firmly established order. For Propertius, this order is identical with mythology as a unified and unifying system of images. For

Tibullus it blends into one with the simple customs and occupa-
tions of country life as reflections of a distant Golden Age. For
Catullus, here at least, it is Roman religion with its give and
take, which provides something permanent, although it may not
appeal to the imagination.

Catullus felt that the poet still had the authority to answer the
greater human questions. It was not enough to analyse human
emotions, as the Alexandrian poets had done, nor was it possible
for him to go on forever, detaching small pieces of existence and
dealing with them as an artist. His life had reached a turning-
point, his emotional balance was deeply disturbed and he had to
accept defeat. But now, even more clearly than ever before, the
voice of the true poet goes on with its music which makes loss
and disgrace seem beautiful.

Catullus' influence on the elegiac poets of the Augustan age is
considerable, even though it was impossible fifteen or twenty
years after Catullus' death to recreate the spirit of adventure
which had animated the 'modern poets', Catullus and his friends,
in their search for a new poetic idiom. And those forms which
were most flexible in Catullus' hands, the *nugae*, were discarded
by the Augustan poets in favour of the more ambitious forms of
ode and elegy.

Whe Catullus began to write, he had before him the 'objective' mythological elegies of the Alexandrians as well as their
short informal epigrams. Their learned elegies dealt with the
loves of heroes and heroines of the past. In their epigrams they
talked about their own love-affairs, but in a light-handed, not-
too-serious manner. It almost seems as though Meleager and
Callimachus tried at all costs to avoid the suspicion that they
might be utterly the slaves of love. Just when they are about to
be serious, they add a touch of irony – 'romantic irony' – and
dissolve, as it were, the impact of their own confession.

Here again Catullus broke through the convention. He experimented with both forms, the long learned elegy and the epigram;
but he did not simply imitate the Alexandrians. He wrote about
himself, his friends, his mistress; but he treated them as human
beings, not as stereotyped pieces on the chequer-board of the
social game. Roman love-poetry begins with Catullus, because he
takes love seriously. Lesbia is not a Greek courtesan; she is a

lady. He reverses the relationship between man and woman which the Greek epigrammatists took for granted. Lesbia is the *domina*, 'mistress', in the true sense of the word; and he, her lover and slave, depends on her whims and moods. The Hellenistic poets reserved such an exalted status for the heroines of the past or (as in Antimachus' *Lyde* and Parthenius' funeral elegy on Arete) for their wives after death. A living Phryne or Heliodora did not rate this honour.

4

The Art of Tibullus

'Je veux, dans mes derniers adieux,
Disait Tibulle à son amante,
Attacher mes yeux sur tes yeux,
Te presser de ma main mourante.'

Mais quand on sent qu'on va passer,
Quand l'âme fuit avec la vie,
A-t-on des yeux pour voir Délie,
Et des mains pour la caresser?
— VOLTAIRE, *A Madame Lullin*

Two texts appended to the manuscripts of Tibullus tell us little of his life: (1) an epigram which is usually attributed to Domitius Marsus, though the name appeared only, according to J. J. Scaliger (1577) in the lost *Fragmentum Cuiacianum*; (2) an anonymous *Vita Tibulli*, no doubt the work of a medieval compiler who may have used a lost chapter in Suetonius' *De Poetis*.

Horace addresses an Albius whom most scholars take to be Albius Tibullus in two poems, *Carm.* 1.33 and *Epist.* 1.4. The tone of both poems is friendly and slightly patronizing, as if an older man were speaking to a younger friend.

Ovid, born in 43 B.C., mentions Tibullus as one of his predecessors (*Trist.* 4.10.51-4). They never knew each other intimately, but Ovid wrote an elegy on Tibullus' death (*Amores* 3.9).

According to the epigram mentioned above, Vergil and Tibullus were 'companions' in death. Since Vergil died in 19 B.C., scholars have until recently assumed that Tibullus died in the same year. An interval of one or two years is not impossible. There are reasons to believe that Tibullus wrote 2.5 in 17 B.C.; he may have died in that year, still *iuvenis*, i.e. not yet forty.

If we combine all these clues, we can say that he was born after 65 and before 43, probably around 57 B.C. This would make him slightly older than Propertius. He seems to have been of equestrian rank and his family must have been well-to-do. The poet's references to his *paupertas* should not be taken too seriously; they are little more than literary convention; the erotic poet had to be penniless by definition. Horace, in an epistle addressed to Tibullus, reminds him that

> . . . *di tibi formam,*
> *di tibi divitias dederunt artemque fruendi,*

'the gods gave you good looks, the gods gave you riches and the art of enjoying them.'

(Horace, Epist. 1.4.6f)

One of the main themes of Tibullus' poetry is his need to live in the country. In the earliest elegy of Book I, he prepares himself reluctantly to leave the idyllic surroundings he loves and to embark on his first military campaign (1.10). As a Roman knight he would be obliged to serve in the army for a period of several years.

Thanks to personal connexions, it seems, he was invited to join M. Valerius Messalla Corvinus, the orator, statesman and patron of the letters, when he was sent to Aquitania by Augustus. During this campaign, Tibullus served on Messalla's staff and shared his tent. He took part in Messalla's victory over the Aquitanians and was rewarded with *militaria dona*, 'orders of distinction', if we are to believe the anonymous *Vita Tibulli*. When he celebrates the event in an elegy, written soon afterwards (Tibullus 1.7), he reminds Messalla with a certain modest pride that

> *non sine me est tibi partus honos,*

'not without me have you gained honour.'

(v. 9)

But he felt his military duties as a burden, and the life of action and conquest as a menace to everything he cherished. It seems sadly ironical that he, the most sensitive of the elegiac poets, had to spend so many years of his short life in military camps, away from home. He went to Palestine and Tyre; he saw the Cydnus,

Taurus and the Nile, the Pyrenees and the Rhône,[1] but the exotic appeal of foreign cities and rivers did not relieve his nostalgia for the simple pleasures of the Italian country life.

In Messalla, Tibullus had found a generous, devoted and tactful friend and patron. More than a third of his poems express his gratitude in one way or another. He was not the only poet among Messala's protégés (the *Corpus Tibullianum* contains the works of some minor figures), but he was the most prominent.

His two published books of elegies show us how a cultured Roman nobleman of the Augustan age spent his days of leisure. There is a country-estate, there are some friends (friendship is one of the important things in Messalla's life), and there is a great deal of good conversation: on love, on literature, on past wars, but apparently very little on politics. Tibullus' ideal of life is Epicurean in the best sense of the word, and if he had any doubts as to the validity of such an ideal, Horace's gently teasing verse-epistle (Horace, *Epist.* 1.4) may have dispersed them.

This letter captures one aspect of Tibullus' personality, as his close friends saw it. Here is Tibullus, a young man of means, good-looking, interested in literature (Horace calls him 'fair critic of my satires', v. 1) and generally enjoying life in a civilized manner.

In the other poem which Horace addressed to his young friend (*Odes* 1.33), we find a different Tibullus. He is now in love with a girl, the 'cruel Glycera', *immitis Glycera*, and writes *miserabiles elegi*, 'elegiac laments', because she is unfaithful to him. These may have been his earliest poems, but they are not preserved; perhaps he destroyed them later, when he had found his own personal tone.

Horace has seen the two domains of Tibullus' art, love and the country life. The two are not really separate; for life in the country is twice as attractive in Delia's company, and Tibullus' best poems are those which convey that enjoyment of love in idyllic surroundings. They represent a blend of the pastoral and the elegiac romance, without the strong colours of Theocritus or the exuberance of Propertius.

The poet seems to be haunted by an ever present sense of loss,

[1] On the military campaigns in which Tibullus participated, see Hirschfeld, *Kleine Schriften*, p. 214; Hanslik, RE 8A. 148-150.

of having been robbed of some irretrievable happiness. Neither country life nor love is ever felt as a secure possession. Even when he pictures himself on his farm, absorbed by the rhythm of work and holidays, there is a note of longing in his description, He longs for the Age of Saturn, when the world was innocent. when no ships crossed the seas in quest of wealth, when no strife divided men, no boundaries the fields. This distant realm of well-being becomes the justification of all his dreams.

The last elegy of Book I is one of the earliest poems of Tibullus that we have. In mood and style it corresponds already to his later works. Many of its themes are taken up by the introductory piece (1.1). Together they seem to formulate Tibullus' view of himself as a man and as an artist, and of his place in a world dominated by greed and distrust. Introduction and epilogue answer each other, and the end leads back to the beginning, thus assuring the unity of the book.

The antithesis of war and peace is taken up in another elegy, 1.3 Tibullus, attacked by a sudden illness, had to be left behind on the island of Corcyra while Messalla and his army sailed on. Again there is a strong contrast between the poet's real situation (being sick and lonely and far from home) and his dreams of love and bucolic happiness.

This sentimental and pathetic elegy is followed by a not-too-serious piece of writing which toys with literary conventions dear to the Alexandrians. 1.4 is a blend of the subjective love-elegy and the didactic poem. Its theme is rather unique in the history of the Latin elegy. As a whole, it relieves the note of despair and unrequited longing that made itself heard more and more urgently from 1.2 to 1.3. After declaring in the preceding poems his devotion to Delia, Tibullus now claims to be in love with a handsome boy, Marathus. He needs advice and listens to a long lecture on homosexual love delivered by the god Priapus himself.

In the two following elegies, he returns to Delia. Both 1.5 and 1.6 belong closely together. Certain motives of 1.1 and 1.2 reappear once more. But by now Tibullus has realized the impossibility of achieving a lasting happiness with Delia. What had always been a dream, nothing but a promise of fulfilment, seems now more distant than ever.

Delia prefers a wealthy rival to the (supposedly) poor poet. She is unfaithful to him and, what is worse, he himself has taught her the methods of deceit she now uses against him. He feels he could forgive her once more for the sake of her old mother (a sentimental touch unparalleled in the history of the Roman love-elegy); once more he is holding out his hand to her, but he knows only too well that she does not need the devotion which he had offered so freely.

The next elegy (1.7), a gratulatory poem in the Hellenistic manner, celebrates Messalla. Written in honour of his triumph over the Aquitanians, it is also a birthday poem. History and imagination, reality and poetic vision are blended into one. Tibullus conjures up the exotic landscapes which have seen him at Messalla's side. The poem concludes and crowns, as it were, the series of Messalla-poems in Book I.

The following two elegies, 1.8 and 1.9, are παίγνια, 'playful pieces', in the manner of 1.4. Their half-frivolous, half-conventional mood contrasts with the learned, heavily ornamented style of the seriously intended 1.7.

The Book was probably edited as a whole by Tibullus himself, no doubt soon after 27 B.C., the accepted date for 1.7. But originally each poem may have circulated separately. When he had a sufficient number of poems to fill a book, he was faced with the problem of arrangement. He might have placed them in a chronological order, but chose instead a subtler and, to his mind, more significant principle of arrangement.

It is the principle of ποικιλία, variatio, whose purpose is to enhance the character of the single poem by its contrast with those preceding and following it. This may be a contrast of mood or style, of content or metre. Horace, for example, in the first poems of his first book of Odes, displays the various metrical systems which he has at his command. For the Latin elegiac poets the metre and, as a rule, the woman they celebrate remain the same throughout the book. But there is a wide range of moods and situations, from the serious to the humorous, from the tragic to the debonair.

The arrangement of the poems in Book II follows a similar line, although it is not as clearly marked as in Book I. Some of the early themes reappear: the poet in love, the poet as a friend, a gentleman farmer, a student of Roman antiquities. It has been said that the book has an unfinished look. It is certainly much smaller than Book I, but there are no clear signs that 2.5 has not been revised for publication and that the whole book was carelessly put together by a posthumous editor.

Nemesis, the woman to whom it is devoted, but not dedicated, was his last love. At Tibullus' death, she is *cura recens*, a 'recent passion' (Ovid, *Amores* 3.9.32). Her name is absent from the first two poems, but a significant passage in 2.1 suggests that the poet is in love once more:

> a miseri quos hic graviter deus urget! at ille
>   felix, cui placidus leniter afflat Amor.

'O wretched they whom this god (Love) violently attacks! But lucky is he who enjoys the gentle breeze of peaceful Love.'

(Tibullus 2.1.79f)

Soon we are told more about the poet's new affair, which has been going on for a year, according to 2.5,

> iaceo cum saucius annum . . .
> usque cano Nemesim . . .

'while I lie stricken with love for a whole year . . . I sing of Nemesis incessantly . . .'

(Tibullus 2.5.109, 111)

She typifies the cold selfish courtesan; she is even less faithful than Delia. Her relationship with the poet is a brief, violent and sensual *capriccio*. For this very reason it has, perhaps, more vividness than the Delia-romance. Certain episodes, such as the death of Nemesis' younger sister (2.6.29-40), are probably not mere fiction.

Tibullus' new 'realism' is tangible in the first elegy of Book II, a poem of celebration dedicated to Messalla. Its style is still Alexandrian, not unlike 1.7, but its themes are Roman. A description of the *Ambarvalia*, a Roman country festival, serves as the point of departure for a praise of country life in general. Little is left of the idyllic Arcadian mood of 1.1 and 1.10. The *vita rustica* is now envisaged as the sum of many concrete details.[1]

The following elegy, 2.2, is a birthday poem, a favourite form of composition in Messalla's circle. A few years ago Tibullus had dealt with similar themes (1.7), on a higher plane, and in a richer orchestration. The new style of the second book, and especially of 2.2, conveys a fresh impression of sweet health, comparable in painting to the *Nozze Aldobrandini*, whose subdued colours and unbroken outlines seem like an illustration for Tibullus' elegy.

The themes of 1.1 and 1.10 reappear in a modified form in 2.3. Tibullus is tired of the city life and of military exploits. To him they are the symbols of the *hubris* of his time. In a moving passage (vv. 35-46), he laments the passing away of the Golden Age of innocence. His sense of loss is sharpened by a distressing personal experience. Nemesis, his mistress, has followed her new lover to a house in the country. In order to be near her, Tibullus is ready to work as a labourer in the fields.

The poems 4 and 6 belong together. Tibullus longs for Nemesis, but she scorns his poetry and prefers the gifts offered to her by the poet's wealthy rivals. She tortures Tibullus by her fickleness and selfishness. Now he would like to be rich to give her what she desires. Now he hurls threats at the *lena*, the 'bawd' or 'go-between' who, he believes, has caused his predicament. The last of the Nemesis-poems, 2.6, ends on a note of sadness and quiet despair.

These two poems are separated by a congratulatory hymn for M. Valerius Messallinus, Messalla's son, written on his election to the board of the *Quindecimviri*. Like 1.7 and 2.1, it conjures up visions that are highly coloured and exciting. The descriptions are so concrete that they might be modelled after actual works of art. The beginning of the poem, for example, seems like an ἔκφρασις, a rhetorical description of the statue of Apollo on the Palatine, Scopas' masterpiece that we know from Roman coins. This technique reminds one of Propertius; and the 'praise of Rome' (vv. 19-66) seems to foreshadow Propertius' Roman elegies.

As a poet Tibullus stands halfway between Propertius and Vergil. With Propertius he shares some typical erotic motifs;

[1] On this poem cf. the doctoral dissertation of P. Poestgens (Diss. Kiel 1940). The same theme had been treated by Vergil, *Georgica* 1.338ff.

with Vergil he shares the feeling for nature and country life. But his love-experience is not that of Propertius, and his bucolic themes are not those of Vergil.

In order to escape from the harsh reality of his time, Vergil had created an ideal world, the Arcadia of his shepherds. Tibullus feels at home in this world, but hesitates to populate it with Vergil's (and Theocritus') concrete characters and events. There is a certain robustness and solidity in Vergil which we do not find in Tibullus. Compared to Vergil, Tibullus is neither a story-teller nor a dramatist, but a lyric poet in the modern sense of the word. In his poetry the reality of the Italian countryside loses its strong colours and blends imperceptibly with the scenery. We feel the keen delight that a familiar landscape must have given to the poet after a long absence abroad.

At the same time, this scenery becomes the symbol of a world beyond reality, a world that is not shackled by bonds of time and space. Trees, springs, the half-forgotten statues of country-gods are alive in a mysterious way. A short walk around his farm becomes for Tibullus a journey to a land unknown at the far end of the earth. Legend and history are a haunting presence all around him.

In one of his earliest published poems (1.10), Tibullus is haunted by the fear of being separated from the idyllic surroundings that mean so much to him. After the disillusionment of his first real love-affair, he finds comfort and rest again in the country (2.1). He is older and more mature by now. What seemed to be a fragile dream in 1.1 and 1.10 has become more tangible in 2.1; what was once seen through a golden haze is now more vivid and moves at a quicker pace. In the celebration of the *Ambarvalia* he feels the presence of the moral and religious forces that made Rome what it is.

Still he is attracted above all to the picturesque views and customs of country life. The country fairs, the shepherds' games, appeal to his imagination. In these simple pleasures the early life of mankind is reflected, not as a struggle for survival, but as a natural equilibrium between work and play.

The farmer's life is also the true revelation of certain essentially Roman virtues, such as *pietas*. Tibullus' own religious feeling is deeply rooted in his love for the countryside. It has nothing of Ovid's bland scepticism or Propertius' Alexandrian glamour. As Tibullus lies sick in Corcyra, he invokes the *patrii lares*. Propertius, in a similar situation, would have conjured up all the major and minor deities (*dique deaeque omnes* . . .) of the Greek Pantheon in addition to some obscure local gods. Tibullus' *naïveté* is perhaps not as simple as he wants us to believe. The invocation of Roman gods such as Pales, Silvanus, Ceres, may be just as 'literary' as the crowd of nymphs and heroes which populate Propertius' imagination. But after the vogue of Alexandrian poetry at Rome, during which these motifs had been very nearly worn out, Tibullus' discovery of the poetic values in Roman religion is refreshing.

Tibullus' religious feeling is less representative, less 'official' than that of Horace or Vergil. On the whole, the poets of Messalla's circle are not as deeply concerned with great religious and national issues as the protégés of Maecenas. It is no coincidence that Tibullus likes to dwell on the concept of the *genius*, a personification of the individual. Whenever he deals with a subject that transcends his own personal experience, he seems a little ill at ease. In such cases he relies more than usually on literary reminiscences and borrows more freely from Alexandrian poetry in order to sustain his waning enthusiasm (for example, in the poem for Messallinus, 2.5).

On the other hand, Tibullus is too much of a Roman to approach religion as a purely emotional experience. Roman religion was by no means a mystic relationship with the infinite; it was almost an exact science, with strict rules fixed by tradition. In his accounts of religious festivals and rites he is well aware of this. He takes great care in enumerating country-gods (1.1.15ff). He is delighted when he sees a half-forgotten stone adorned with flowers by an unknown worshipper (1.1.12). He is interested in foreign gods. Once he invokes Isis (1.3.27f), but hesitates to promise her any offerings and leaves this duty to Delia. His hymn to Osiris (1.7.27ff) is literary in character, a triumph of learned poetry, not a document of personal religiosity.

Less than a hundred years after his death Tibullus was already considered as a classic of the love-elegy. Quintilian, in his handbook of rhetoric, admits that some critics still prefer Propertius, but states openly that, to his own (neo-classical) taste, Tibullus is *tersus atque elegans maxime . . . auctor*, ' a most polished and elegant author'. This was not a revolutionary statement. Although Propertius was still alive when Tibullus died, Domitius Marsus proclaimed that now the love-elegy had lost its master. And Ovid, shortly afterward, prophesied that

> donec erunt ignes arcusque Cupidinis arma,
> discentur numeri, culte Tibulle, tui.

'as long as flames and the bow are the arms of Cupid, your rhythms, elegant Tibullus, will be a model.'

(Ovid, Amores 1.15.27f)

'Elegant Tibullus' – this epithet has caught the very essence of Tibullus' art. It is unostentatious and subtle; it avoids emphasis, the striking phrase, Propertius' kind of realism, Ovid's kind of brilliance. But it is art nonetheless, one that aims at vividness without effect, at the phrase that is not startling but haunts the mind. All these qualities are suggested by *cultus*; and Ovid, who applied this epithet to Tibullus, is not the only reader to admire them.

Tibullus' style is less exuberant than that of Propertius. Some critics have called him 'anaemic' and suggested that he lacked creative vitality. But his simplicity is not a sign of poverty; it is the result of conscious restraint. His manner of writing is that which the Alexandrian critics termed the λεπταὶ ῥήσιες, the 'slender style'.[1] Horace finds the same quality in his own manner, when he speaks of the 'slender spirit' which the Muse gave to him:

> spiritum Graiae tenuem Camenae
> Parca non mendax dedit.

(Horace, Odes 2.16.38)

Presumably this is one of the reasons why he was more attracted to Tibullus than to Propertius. Both Tibullus and Horace prefer the lucid to the flamboyant, the simple to the bombastic.

Unlike Propertius, Tibullus never claims to be a Roman Callimachus. Actually his style is much closer to that of the Alexandrian poet. Without an ambitious display of learning, without talking

---

[1] On the difference between the 'sublime' and the 'humble' style in ancient literary criticism, see the excellent remarks of F. Wehrli, in *Phyllobolia Von der Mühll* (Basel 1946), 9ff.

as much about the secrets of his craft as Propertius, Tibullus' style reveals the careful effort of an intelligent and sensitive writer. He knows that he must abandon everything that is not authentically his own. Once he has realized that 'delicate phrases' (Callimachus' ideal of style)[1] are his natural form of expression, he refuses to experiment with the Latin language in the Propertian manner.

He avoids colloquialisms (there are many in Catullus and Propertius) and adjectives or adverbial expressions which have a conversational ring.[2] It often seems as if Tibullus had anticipated the later development of Augustan poetry toward greater purity. He also refuses the all-too-facile sentimental undertones that have become by that time inseparable from certain words or wordforms. Catullus called Lesbia *mea lux*, and Cynthia is to Propertius *mea vita*. To Tibullus these terms of endearment must have sounded trite. He says *mea Delia* – but what a subtle melody these two words bring to his line!

Tibullus ignores a large part of the conventional erotic terminology. He has weeded out such expressions as *deliciae, medulla, libido, nequitia, ludere, lusus, perire*, and many other half-playful conceits that had lost their vigour by frequent use. They either dramatize love (*libido, perire*) or prettify it (*ludere, nequitia*), two extremes that are equally suspect to Tibullus. The associations of these terms had, by now, become too obvious; they invariably added a false note to the precise thought or experience which the poet wanted to convey.

Tibullus' imagery shows the same economy of means. He prefers sober similes and avoids monumental, grandiose or farfetched images. Because of their very simplicity his images often have a full-blown enchanting sweetness found nowhere else in Latin poetry. Once, in two lines, he tells the reader that he cannot bear to be separated from Delia:

> *asper eram et bene discidium me ferre loquebar,*
> *at mihi nunc longe gloria fortis abest.*

[1] Cf. Callimachus, *Epigr.* 27 (Pf.); E. Reitzenstein, in *Festschrift R. Reitzenstein* (1931), 25ff.

[2] There is a very readable study of Tibullus' *elegantia* by R. Bürger, in *Charites Friedrich Leo* (1911), 371ff; his results have been modified by B. Axelson, *Unpoetische Wörter* (Lund 1945), 114ff.

'I was harsh and said I could easily bear the separation, but now that valiant boast is far away from me.'

(Tibullus 1.5.1f)

He uses simple, straightforward words, with the exception, perhaps, of the unexpected *fortis*, but this is certainly a very unobtrusive image. Propertius, in the same situation, describing a similar mood, crowds a great deal more into his distich:

> *liber eram et vacuo meditabar vivere lecto,*
> *at me composita pace fefellit Amor.*

'I was free and considered living without a mistress, but though the truce was made, Love deceived me.'

(Propertius 2.2.1f)

Both couplets are very similar in their structure (*asper eram – liber eram*, *loquebar – meditabar*, *at mihi – at me*). Propertius wrote most of the poems of his second book at a time when Tibullus' Book I had already been published. It is highly probable that he knew this passage and tried, consciously or not, to compete with it, to outdo it.

This is only one example among many which might be quoted. In each case Propertius seems more decorative and intense, while Tibullus is trying to find the perfect form for his simple lucid statement. In Propertius, inanimate things become alive and talk – the house door (1.16), the dead soldier (1.21), the ghosts of Cornelia (4.11) and of Cynthia (4.7). His complex, intense, urgent, and probing poems can excite us in spite of the roughness of their form or their discordant passages. Tibullus has set himself a more difficult task. He wants to move the reader by the discreet gesture, the *sotto voce* of his appeal.

It is a pleasure to read a Roman poet who does not for one moment assume the strained posture of the bard in full attire, lyre in hand, on a pedestal, straining under seemingly enormous burdens. Tibullus believes in the principle of *ars est celare artem*, 'art consists in concealing art'. Never is the melody of his verse drowned in the clanking and rattling of the literary machinery. But it is precisely because of his studied literary cultivation and knowledge that his works read as if they owed nothing to conscious literary technique.

His style is that of the best passages in Terence. It can be described by two terms, *urbanitas* and *elegantia*. While the style of Terence reflects the highly civilized way of life in Scipio's circle, Tibullus owes a great deal to his association with Messalla, *Latini sermonis observator diligentissimus*, 'the most careful observer of Latin speech' (Seneca Rhetor, *Controv.* 2.4.8). He induces the reader to listen to his soliloquies as if their effect were of no concern to him.

Tibullus may lead us through a long cycle of loosely connected themes (as in 1.1), where successive scenes and images blend into each other and seem to have no logical relation, yet dictate to us what we are to feel and carry us gently from one mood to the next. Unlike Ovid, he is unwilling to divide his imagination into tight compartments by subordinating a series of ideas to a clearly stated proposition. All his themes are of equal importance to him.

His poems should be read aloud; only then will they reveal their undulating rhythm, their exquisite elegiac cadence. Each couplet is an artistic unit, because the regular pattern of the second half of his pentameters has much the same effect as rhyme. It seems difficult to describe Tibullus' metrical art more persuasively than W. Y. Sellar in his book on *Horace and the Elegiac Poets*:

'The sense of each distich is complete in itself. . . . The clauses are direct and simple . . . and follow each other without any connecting word, or with a conjunction co-ordinating them with one another, or more rarely marking the dependence of one thought on another. . . . There is an equable balance between the first and second half of the pentameter. . . . To a modern ear the movement of the verse is smoother than that of the Ovidian elegiac with its rapid succession of epigrammatic antithesis: while it never leaves the impression of strain and labour, as if the single lines and couplets were beat out by separate efforts, which is often left by the metre of Propertius.'

5

Alexandrian Themes in Tibullus

Wie der wechselnde Wind nach allen Seiten die hohen
Saaten im weichen Schwung niedergebogen durchwühlt:
Liebekranker Tibull! so unstet fluten, so reizend
Deine Gesänge dahin, während der Gott dich bestürmt.
— EDUARD MÖRIKE

Propertius praises Callimachus and Philetas as the masters of the elegy and claims that they are his models. Tibullus never mentions the name of any Greek (or, for that matter, Roman) poet. But the fact that he fails to acknowledge his debt to any predecessors does not mean that they did not exist nor that he did not know them.

To be a *poeta doctus* implied a thorough knowledge of Greek literature and mythology. There is very little mythology in Tibullus and, unlike Propertius, he avoids precious allusions and literary references. This absence of erudition and the lack of the purely decorative element in Tibullus is with rare exceptions so strict and consistent, that it seems characteristic of his art.

He has been called the 'most original' of the elegiac love-poets. This term is partly justified, partly wrong. It is correct to say that his objective as an artist was to be 'original'. He refused to be identified with a group such as the *cantores Euphorionis* or the poets around Maecenas. His association with Messalla was informal and, at the same time, intimate enough to leave him all the personal freedom he wanted and needed.

In his dependence on the classical and Alexandrian tradition in

83

Greek poetry he is hardly more 'original' than either Propertius or Ovid. This has been shown sufficiently by the recent discoveries of Greek literary papyri. Unlike Propertius, he never claimed to be the Roman Callimachus, nor does he outline his literary programme as decidedly as Propertius. But he was at least as familiar with Callimachus' work as Propertius, to whom the Alexandrian poet was, above all, a great and glamorous name, surrounded by romantic, almost religious associations.

During his short life, Tibullus retained the freshness, the melancholy, the wonder and curiosity of youth. If he never declared explicitly that the Alexandrian poets (and Callimachus in particular), were necessary to him as pacemakers and criteria for his development, this does not mean that they had no influence on his verse. To identify all the Alexandrian motifs in Tibullus would be impossible, even today, with our comparatively extensive knowledge of Alexandrian poetry. Moreover, an accumulation of parallels and literary reminiscences, as necessary as it might be in view of a new commentary on Tibullus (we need one!), would rather obscure the issue than show the clear outlines that we postulate for him. We shall limit ourselves, within this survey, to two poems, 1.7 and 1.4. Although they are not 'typical' for Tibullus, the evidence they offer is particularly suggestive.

In 27 B.C., Messalla celebrated his triumph over the Aquitanians.[1] For this occasion, Tibullus composed an elegy (1.7). It is one of the most complex poems he has written, because it does not fit into any of the traditional categories of literary criticism. Apparently, it has no unified structure, no straightforward thematic development. Past and present, myth and reality, blend into each other, following each other without any visible order, and carrying the reader through a range of various moods.

The elegy begins as a birthday poem (1-2); then, with an ingenious transition (a *vaticinium ex eventu*, 3-4), becomes a triumphal song (5-8), only to turn into an autobiographical narrative (the poet looks back on the campaigns that led him at Messalla's side into many countries, 9-22).

V. 23 marks a new beginning. The following thirty-two lines

[1] On Messalla's triumph and its date see A. Degrassi, ed., *Inscr. Ital.* XIII 1 (1947), p. 571; R. Hanslik, RE 8A.149ff.

(exactly half of the poem) are a hymn to Osiris. The introduction of this Egyptian god who is celebrated as a hero of civilization is prepared by the vision of the Nile (22). Osiris is invited to take part in Messalla's birthday celebration (49-54).

This leads us back to the present occasion itself and to the man, Messalla, who is being honoured. A vision of Messalla's offspring, of the Via Latina which he repaired, of the people's grateful memory, and a brief prayer addressed to the *Natalis* – these are the themes that conclude, in rapid sequence, this unusual poem.

What makes it so unusual, is its combination of various literary *genera*. It begins as a birthday poem, turns almost imperceptibly into a triumphal ode, then becomes a religious hymn, and ends, more conventionally, as a birthday poem.

In the history of the elegy, we find parallels for each of these components. There are several Greek birthday poems in the elegiac metre by younger contemporaries of Tibullus,[1] but this form of literature may have been more popular than our extant examples suggest. The later handbooks of rhetoric contain precepts for birthday orations which might be applied to verse as well as to prose.[2] The poets of Messalla's circle were particularly fond of the elegiac γενεθλιακόν; Tibullus wrote another one (2.2 for Cornutus), and there are two companion-pieces in the 'Garland of Sulpicia' (*Corp. Tibull.* 3.11 and 3.12).

A victory ode was traditionally in the lyric mode, but war, victory and heroic death were already themes of the archaic Greek elegy. Victorious athletes had been at all times celebrated in elegiac distichs, destined to be engraved on the bases of honorary statues. Callimachus' elegies on the victory or victories of Sosibius were, perhaps, nothing more than an experiment; it seems likely, at any rate, as we shall see below, that Tibullus knew them.

---

[1] Before Tibullus' time, we have only two Greek birthday poems, neither of which is typical; Hedylus (quoted by Athenaeus, IV, p. 176D) is actually an epitaph and Callimachus, *Iambus* XII (cf. C. M. Dawson, *Yale Class. Stud.*, 1950, 116ff), is half satirical.

[2] Pseudo-Dionysius of Halicarnassus, *Ars Rhet.* 3 (pp. 266ff, Us.-Rad.), Menand. Rhet., in Spengel, *Rhet. Graec.* III, p. 412f. Neither Cicero nor Quintilian mentions birthday orations. Tibullus' poem seems to be free of any rhetorical influence, see F. Levy, *Stud. Ital. Filol. Class.* (1929), 104, n. 1; 110f.

Hymns addressed to the gods are traditionally in hexameters (the so-called Homeric hymns and all but one of Callimachus' hymns), but Callimachus experimented at least once with the elegiac metre. Such hymns might be in the form of an ἀρεταλογία, a praise of the god's 'virtues' or blessings. An example (also in the elegiac manner) is Propertius 3.17; another (from Messalla's circle) Lygdamus 6, both addressed to Dionysus. It is interesting that Tibullus, in 1.7, praises Osiris as the god of wine (vv. 33ff) and identifies his gift to mankind with that of Bacchus (vv. 39-40, 41-42).

Another type of the religious hymn is the ὕμνος κλητικός, an invitation to the god to join the celebration. Its earliest form seems to have been the lyric poem and one of the first epigrammatic versions of this motif (Nossis, *Anth. Pal.* 6.265) still shows strong lyrical influence.[1] But the motif itself found its way into elegiac love-poetry (Posidippus, *Anth. Pal.* 12.131, is an example; Aphrodite is invited to come 'in gracious mood' to a courtesan) and in the social poetry of Messalla's circle it almost became a commonplace.[2]

All these parallels do not really 'explain' Tibullus' elegy 1.7. What is new here is the combination of all these elements. One can only compare it to Catullus 68, where, between a more or less conventional prologue and epilogue, various apparently unrelated themes (the poet's love for Lesbia, the mythological love-story of Laodamia and Protesilaus, the Trojan War, the death of Catullus' brother) follow each other in this sequence, to be resumed, in the second half of the poem, in the reverse order.

Both elegies are more than a casual series of picturesque images or sentimental themes. Because they are so singular, they seem to have the character of an experiment. But it is possible to point out the sequence that underlies the apparent *beau désordre*. The poetic imagination bridges time and space. Both Catullus and Tibullus re-live and idealize important moments of their life. In order to say all they want to say, they have to create a new medium by a fusion of the traditional ones.

[1] Cf. *Anth. Pal.* 6.273, 'in the manner of Nossis'; Horace c. 1.30; R. Reitzenstein, *Neue Jahrb.* (1908), 81ff; E. Norden, *Agnostos Theos* (1913), 168ff; R. Pfeiffer's note on Callimachus, fr. 299; G. Luck, *Mus. Helv.* (1954), 185.

[2] Cf. Tibullus 1.7.49 and 53; 2.5.2; Pseudo-Tibullus 3.8 and 3.10.

It is very doubtful whether we shall ever find in Greek poetry an exact parallel for this method of fusion. The Roman elegists must have felt that this was their own contribution. If they embodied Alexandrian themes into this framework, they made them into something new. The reader was expected to recognize the old themes and also to admire the new significance which they gained within a new context.

After this brief survey of the elegy as a whole, we may be permitted to concentrate on its middle part, the hymn to Osiris. It seems to be a poem within a poem, and yet it would be impossible to cut from its context and still have a complete birthday poem or a complete victory song. It contains many reminiscences from Callimachus; hence, it is characteristic of the way in which Tibullus handles his material.

The hymn to Osiris (vv. 27-54) is prepared by a vision of the Nile (vv. 22-27), appearing as the last example in a fairly long list of rivers which symbolize all the countries that Messalla (and Tibullus) saw during their campaigns.[1] The glory of his triumph will be for ever associated with the places that witnessed his victories – this seems to be the implicit meaning of this geographical excursus.

The Nile itself is first described objectively. During the most intense heat period, it carries an abundant supply of water.

> quid? referam . . .
>
> . . .
>
> qualis et arentes cum findit Sirius agros,
>   fertilis aestiva Nilus abundet aqua.

'What? should I tell[2] how, in the summer, when Sirius splits the parched fields, the life-giving Nile overflows with water?'

(vv. 17, 21f)

The observation is not new; many visitors to Egypt had made it before Tibullus. Even if he had never seen the Nile himself, he

[1] The military events seem to be listed in chronological order, cf. R. Helm, *Philol. Wochenschr.* (1925), 113; on the picturesque description of the rivers cf. F. Levy, *Gnomon* (1927), 499.

[2] This is a form of the *praeteritio* that is characteristic of the hymnic style. The poet is at a loss (ἀπορία) which of the visions that crowd his imagination he should record.

might have found this piece of information in a geographical handbook. On the other hand, he might have borrowed it from Callimachus, who lived in Egypt and was fond of referring to Egyptian places and customs in his poems. In one of them, also a triumphal song, he speaks of the Nile

θηλύτατον καὶ Νεῖλος ἄγων ἐνιαύσιον ὕδωρ

'and the Nile, carrying every year its fertilizing water.'
(Callimachus, fr. 384.27, Pf.)

In Tibullus, the Nile (identified, as we shall see later, with Osiris himself) takes on a larger importance. It is elevated to the rank of a life-giving principle. Callimachus' line is rather dry and factual; Tibullus, if he knew it, replaced 'every year' more specifically, by 'in the summer', and stressed the blessings of the water by the contrast with the parched field. There is also, in Tibullus, the implication of a kind of cosmic struggle – Sirius, on the one hand, a destructive power; and the Nile, counteracting his influence by his benign gift to mankind.

In the next distich, another Callimachean reminiscence (from the same poem on Sosibius' victory) can be found:

> Nile pater, quanam possim te dicere causa
> aut quibus in terris occuluisse caput?

'Father Nile, for what reason could I say have you hidden your head – or in what regions?'

(v. 23f)

That the sources of the Nile had not been discovered was common knowledge among the poets of the Augustan age.[1] If Tibullus refers to it in this elegy, he could not expect to impress the reader with a rare piece of information. A few lines further down, he may have read in Callimachus' poem:

ὃν οὐδ' ὅθεν οἶδεν ὁδεύω | θνητὸς ἀνήρ

'and no mortal man knows whence I flow.'
(Callimachus, fr. 384.31f)

In Tibullus' context, this motif gains a power which it does not have in the original. It intensifies the atmosphere of mystery

---

[1] Cf. Horace, c. 4.14.45f; Ovid, *Metamorphoses* 2.255, etc.

which surrounds the famous river. In Callimachus' poem, the Nile himself is speaking, and his manner of speech is a little chatty and fatuous. Tibullus dispenses with Callimachus' irony; his tone is more that of a hymn, and the Nile, to him, becomes 'Father Nile', from whose gifts not only Egypt, but all the other Mediterranean countries benefit.

The following distich (v. 25f) resumes the concept of fertility. Egypt does not need rain; it has the Nile. He is, to his country, what *Iuppiter Pluvius* is to Italy.[1] But he is more than that; he is Osiris and Bacchus as well. And here we approach the central theme of Tibullus' elegy.

The understanding of the poem's structure hinges on the interpretation of the following distich (v. 27f):

> te canit atque suum pubes miratur Osirim
> barbara, Memphiten plangere docta bovem.

'The foreign crowd that has been brought up to lament the bull of Memphis, sings of you and worships you as its Osiris.'

These lines are still addressed to 'Father Nile', but they mark a transition to a new theme. The Nile is more than a river, he is an aspect or a manifestation of the great Osiris. Now we understand why Tibullus has created this atmosphere of mystery almost as soon as he mentioned the Nile.

Each of these references to Egyptian geography and customs, taken by itself, may be no more than a curious piece of information. But within the context of the poem, they lead up to the unexpected identification of the Nile with Osiris. Thus the 'Egyptian' part of Tibullus' elegy assumes a coherence that was not visible at first.[2]

Once more, Tibullus has adapted a line from Callimachus. It is quoted out of context by several ancient grammarians because of the strange words which it contains:

> εἰδυῖαι φαλιὸν ταῦρον ἰηλεμίσαι

'having been taught to lament the white bull . . .'

(Callimachus, fr. 383.16, Pf.)

[1] Honigmann, RE 17.564; cf. Housman's note on Lucan 8.829.
[2] In an excellent discussion of this difficult poem, F. Klingner, *Eranos* (1951), 117ff, has given what I believe to be the correct interpretation of this particular passage.

This 'white bull' is Tibullus' *bos Memphites*; he has translated *ἰηλεμίσαι* by *plangere*, and *εἰδυῖαι* by *docta* (a striking use in this context).

This is doubtless a very successful adaptation. Within the context of the whole elegy, the line seems to represent little more than a picturesque detail, meaning something like, 'This is Egypt.' We should note Tibullus' effort to make even this detail as expressive as possible.

In the following distich (v. 29f) he returns to the praise of Osiris, the Egyptian god who has taught agriculture to mankind:

> *primus aratra manu sollerti fecit Osiris*
> *et teneram ferro sollicitavit humum.*

Elsewhere, Demeter is accredited with these gifts (Ovid, *Amores* 3.10.11ff). It seems that Callimachus, in a lost work, dealt specifically with the 'inventor' of agriculture (Callimachus, fr. 811, Pf.) but it is impossible to determine to what degree it may have influenced Tibullus.[1]

On the whole, the 'Egyptian' part of this elegy owes a great deal to Callimachus. Each of the parallels discussed could be explained away; it is their number and rapid sequence that seems significant.

If Tibullus visited Egypt as Messalla's comrade-in-arms, he must have felt the exotic appeal of this strange country, as did so many others before him. But it was in Callimachus that he discovered the meaning of the Egyptian customs. He saw or remembered Egypt through Callimachus' eyes.

He found a birthday poem in Callimachus, one of the two extant examples of this type of poetry in earlier Hellenistic literature. Callimachus' *Iambus* XII was written on the birth of a girl. Appropriately, it starts with an invocation of Artemis. She is

---

[1] In his review of Richard Harder's *Karpokrates von Chalkis und die memphitische Isispropaganda* (Abh. Berlin 1943, phil.-hist. Kl. 14), Professor A. D. Nock, *Gnomon* 21 (1949), 221ff, has dealt with the praises of Isis, as they are known from inscriptional versions, Diodorus Siculus 1.27 and the so-called *Kore Kosmou*. On an inscription from Chalcis (late third century A.D.), Carpocrates is praised as the inventor of dance, the mixing of wine and water, of flutes and pipes. In other words, he is invested with the attributes of Dionysus and Apollo (Nock, p. 221). Through Delia, Tibullus may have known something about Egyptian religion (Nock, p. 227, n. 1), and his hymn to Osiris may well be an adaptation of actual religious texts such as the inscription mentioned above. (Cf. above p. 14).

identical with Ilithyia, the goddess of childbirth, who, in turn, is often associated with the Fates, the goddesses of destiny.

Since Tibullus intends to stress the importance of the day that gave birth to a man whose fate was linked so closely with the destiny of Rome, an invocation to Artemis or Ilithyia would be out of place. Instead, he begins his poem with a vision of the Fates:

> *hunc cecinere diem Parcae fatalia nentes*
> *stamina, non ulli dissoluenda deo . . .*

'this is the day of which the Parcae sung, weaving their fateful threads which are not to be dissolved by any god . . .'

(v. 1f)

Callimachus, too, referred to the Fates in his birthday poem, calling them

> κάλλιστα νήθουσαι
>> (Callimachus, fr. 202.9, Pf.)

Needless to say, the 'beauty' of their weaving should not be taken in a purely aesthetic sense; it must refer to success or distinction. On the other hand, the weaving of the Fates may be called 'beautiful', because it implies a good life.[1]

It is customary for Latin birthday poetry to introduce the *Genius* representing the *individuality* of the person who is being celebrated, just as the Fates represent his more or less *typical*, common destiny. The *Genius* is a Roman concept, but Tibullus personifies it in the Hellenistic manner:

> *illius et nitido stillent unguenta capillo*
> *et capite et collo mollia serta gerat.*

'Perfumes should drip from his shining hair, and on his head and around his neck he should wear soft garlands.'[2]

(v. 51f)

It seems that, once more, Callimachus provided the colours for this description. At the beginning of his best-known work,

---

[1] Even the life of a god or half-god conforms to the law of the Fates, cf. Ovid, *Tristia* 5.3.25f (on Dionysus), a very close imitation of Tibullus' distich.

[2] Tibullus must have been fond of this description; he uses it again, with small changes, in a later birthday poem, 2.2.6-8.

the *Aitia*, he traces back to its origin a certain kind of sacrifice offered to the Graces on Paros. He has a vision of the three goddesses, draped in purple robes, 'their locks always dripping with perfumes',

$$\dot{\alpha}\pi' \; \dot{o}\sigma\tau\lambda\acute{\iota}\gamma\omega\nu \; \delta' \; a\dot{\iota}\grave{\epsilon}\nu \; \ddot{\alpha}\lambda\epsilon\iota\phi a \; \dot{\rho}\acute{\epsilon}\epsilon\iota.$$

(Callimachus, fr. 7.12, Pf.)

If Tibullus had read Callimachus' poem for Sosibios (see above), he was certainly familiar with the *Aitia* and especially with that part which is most often quoted, its beginning. He replaces the Greek Graces by the Roman *Genius*, adapting a Hellenistic motif to a Latin context.

This has been a one-sided and therefore, perhaps, too arbitrary, discussion of a complex poem. It is actually much more than a series of purple patches borrowing from Callimachus. The single 'parallel' proves little or nothing; it is only the relatively high number of Greek themes in a particularly 'Roman' poem, that seems surprising. The skilful manner in which they are adapted and connected opens up a new way to the understanding of Tibullus' elegy. His reminiscences may be purely verbal associations, they may be literary compliments to a great name – but they always fulfil their function within the larger framework of the poem.[1]

Many of Tibullus' elegies are conventional poems without ever being, for this reason, insincere or mediocre. He avoids the device of massive realism and relies on imagery and symbol, even if this restraint seems to weaken the personal character of his poetry. Occasionally, he does make concessions to the literary fashions of his time; in such cases, he depends more strongly on Hellenistic themes.

The literary form of 1.4, the first of the Marathus-poems, is characteristic. The elegy consists of a dialogue between the poet (1-6) and the god Priapus (9-72), followed by an appeal of the poet to his readers (75-80) and a brief soliloquy (81-84).

Priapus was a fashionable god among the *poetae novi*.[2] Valerius

---

[1] Cf., for example, v. 54, *liba et Mopsopio dulcia melle feram*, and Callimachus, fr. 709 (Pf.).

[2] The most important testimonies on Priapus as a literary theme in Rome have been collected by H. Herter, RE 22.1928, 1930f, 1933; cf. also Büchner, RE

Cato, one of the leaders of the school, had a statue of Priapus in his garden; so did Maecenas. It is tempting to assume that the particular Priapus who is the hero of Tibullus' elegy stood in Messalla's garden. As a literary theme, Priapus appears in Catullus (fr. 1), in the so-called *Catalepton* that goes under Vergil's name, and in Horace's *Satires* (1.8). There is a whole collection of Latin *Priapea*, from different periods and by various authors; Tibullus may be one of them (nr. 83).

Tibullus 1.4 differs from this production in at least two respects. First, it is written as a dialogue, a literary form which is, perhaps, more Hellenistic than Roman.[1] Two texts of Callimachus may be compared, one from the *Aitia* (fr. 114, Pf.), a dialogue between the god Apollo (or his statue) and an unknown person; and fr. 199, Pf. (from the *Iambi*), wherein a statue of Hermes is addressed by the lover of a handsome boy.

Second, Priapus plays the role of an adviser for the love-lorn. Again, we known of a Hellenistic treatment of this theme (Theocritus, *Id*. 1.81ff). If Tibullus knew Theocritus' poem, the substitution of Hermes for Priapus explains itself. If he did not know it, he could have modified the Callimachean situation, because Priapus is the son of Hermes, and there is a clear reference in Callimachus' fragment to the latter's ithyphallic character. The fiction of a talking statue of Priapus is well-known from a number of Greek epigrams at the beginning of Book X of the *Palatine Anthology*.

We have seen so far, that the main theme (homosexual love), the structure (dialogue) and the fiction of a talking statue (Priapus) are Hellenistic. It can be shown that most of the poem's secondary themes and much of its imagery are derived from Hellenistic poetry, especially from Callimachus.

The opening prayer is a little ironical. It has a close parallel in Theocritus (*Epigram* 4), but Tibullus uses the motif in a way that seems entirely his own. The god must be flattered right at the

---

8A.1070. On the question of Tibullus' authorship of *Priap.* 83 see Herter, *Rev. Étud. Anc.* (1953), 404f.

[1] This has been suggested by A. W. Allen, *Yale Class. Stud.* 11 (1950), 267. (By an oversight which I regret I have not acknowledged in the first edition C. M. Dawson's important article in Am. Journ. Philol. 1946, 1ff. which was followed by an equally valuable paper in *Yale Class. Stud.* 1950, 1ff.)

beginning, or he might resent the ludicrous description of his appearance (3-6). The description itself may be conventional, but Tibullus has adapted it very skilfully to his theme: 'Why are you so popular with handsome boys – with such looks?'

Priapus opens his speech with a warning: it is all too easy to fall in love, for each boy is attractive in his own way, and for different reasons. In the very same form, this theme appears in a Greek poet who lived under Nero, Straton (*Anth. Pal.* 12.198); but in a more general form it seems to be characteristic of Hellenistic love-poetry.[1]

After this warning Priapus offers some concrete advice. Above all, he says, the lover needs patience (15-20); if you persevere, he adds, the boy will finally 'bend his neck under the yoke' (16). The same image, in a similar context, is found in one of Callimachus' paederastic epigrams (45, Pf.).

Priapus' second piece of advice is a little more blunt. 'Be generous with oaths!' Jupiter does not punish the perjuries of lovers, no matter whether you swear by the arrows of Artemis or by the hair of Athena (21-26). In this short passage there are no less than two reminiscences, direct or indirect, of Callimachus. The belief that the gods do not mind the perjuries of lovers seems to be as old as Hesiod, but had been revived by Callimachus in a famous little poem (*Ep.* 25, Pf.).[2] Second, the image of Artemis, the huntress, in a Roman poet, is probably derived from Callimachus (fr. 96, Pf.); the Roman Diana was no huntress.

The middle part of the elegy contains practical precepts (39-56), all of them variations on the theme *obsequio plurima vincet amor*, 'by giving in, love will conquer most obstacles' (40). This part comes, perhaps, closest to an *ars amatoria* in Ovid's sense.

---

[1] The idea that the lover is attracted not by the qualities of the beloved, but by his or her failings, can be traced back to Plato, *Rep.* 474D/E. Plato draws attention to the fact that to a lover his loved one's failings really seem to be attractions. A man in love with a girl with a squint loves the squint (because it is hers), and the girl because, not in spite of the squint. In Latin poetry, this idea appears for the first time in Lucretius 4.1160ff; cf. also Propertius 2.25.41ff; Ovid, *Amores* 2.4, *Ars Amatoria* 2.657ff; and many other passages collected by A. St. Pease on Cic. *Nat. Deor.* 1.79 (Harvard Univ. Pr. 1956), 1.79.

[2] Cf. Catullus c. 70; Propertius 2.28.8; Ovid, *Amores* 1.8.85f, 2.8.19f, 2.16.43ff, 3.3.11f; Lygdamus 6.49f; Horace c. 2.8 (and the preface of Kiessling-Heinze to this poem).

It is framed by two digressions; one a very beautiful lament on the passing of youth and beauty (27-38); the other, a tragicomical diatribe against the venality of the handsome boys (57-70). For the sake of clarity, I shall deal only with the Hellenistic themes of the latter digression.

It is summarized in the first distich:

> *heu male nunc artes miseras haec saecula tractant:*
> *iam tener adsuevit munera velle puer.*

'Alas, how badly does this century now treat the wretched Arts; a boy in his tender age is already in the habit of demanding gifts.'

(57-58)

This is the point of view of the 'poor poet' who has nothing to offer to his beloved but verse. His diatribe is directed against the 'rich lover', the 'greedy boy', and, in general, the corruption and decadence of the 'century'. Thus it is partly a praise of poetry (61-66), partly an invective against the spirit of materialism which is hostile to poetry and the arts (59-60, 67-70). Each of these themes can be traced back to Hellenistic poetry.

First, the 'poor poet': Callimachus, in one of his erotic epigrams (32, Pf.), admits that he is poor, but resents the fact that Menippus is constantly holding his poverty against him. In two other epigrams (28 and 31, Pf.), Callimachus mentions with contempt those boys who offer themselves to everyone. Elsewhere, in the third *Iambus*, he argues with a boy, Eratosthenes, who sells his favours for hard cash.

After Callimachus, the figure of the 'poor poet' becomes more and more popular in Hellenistic and Roman love-poetry, and its literary treatment invites elaborate comparisons of poetry and material gifts, honesty and greed, true and false love, the simple life and the life of luxury. Even Tibullus, who is well-to-do, claims that he has only poems to offer to his mistress (1.5.67f).

Priapus has no concrete situation in mind. His attack is aimed at all the boys who prefer money to true love – or rather, he curses the 'inventor' of this practice:

> *at tua, qui venerem docuisti vendere primus,*
> *quisquis es, infelix urgeat ossa lapis.*

'Whoever you are who taught for the first time to sell
love, may a cursed stone weigh heavily on your bones.'

(59-60)

Curses directed against the 'first inventor' of something were a
favourite requisite of Hellenistic poets. Callimachus, in the *Lock
of Berenice*, cursed the Chalybes, a nation on the southern shore
of the Black Sea, because they were the first to live by working
iron (fr. 110.48-50, Pf., translated by Catullus, 66.47-50). That
it was dangerous to make any kind of invention, is shown by the
fate of the man who constructed the bull of Phalaris; he became
the first victim of this instrument of torture. (Callimachus told
the story in the *Aitia*.) But literary 'curses' could be aimed at
anyone who, for some reason, had annoyed the poet. Callimachus
and Euphorion were the masters of this literary form. No matter
how trivial the incident – someone had stolen Euphorion's drinking cup – the poet was ready to shower him with learned curses.
There is no exact parallel to Tibullus' distich in the fragments of
Callimachus; but Tibullus was doubtless aware of this literary
motif.

In the following three distichs, Priapus exalts the power of
poetry and urges the *pueri delicati* to love the Muses and their
spokesmen, the poets, for the gifts they have to offer are more
precious than gold. This is a common theme in Latin elegiac
poetry, and we can only guess from its frequency and certain common features that it must be derived from a famous Hellenistic
original.

The subsequent condemnation of those who 'do not listen to
the Muses' (they are identical with those who 'sell their love')
takes a rather unexpected turn (67-70). Instead of cursing them
in the traditional manner, Priapus wishes them to become wor-
shippers of Cybele. He hopes that they will all be driven by their
madness from city to city, and that they will castrate themselves
to the accompaniment of Phrygian flutes.

This is an odd wish. One can understand that the Romans
were struck by the fantastic ritual of this oriental religion. Propertius quotes the self-mutilation that was part of the cult of
Cybele as an example of utter senselessness, a kind of *acte gratuit*
(Propertius 2.22.16). Ovid, in his *Ibis*, wishes that the nameless

enemy, who is the target of that poem, may mutilate himself and, as a eunuch-priest of the *Magna Mater*, beat the tambourine (Ovid, *Ibis* 451-456).

One can understand that Tibullus, Propertius and Ovid considered the orgiastic self-castration to the sound of flute-music as the highest form of perversion. It is a fate they wish on their worst enemy – but why on the enemy of poetry? A fragment of Callimachus provides the answer. He has contrasted, in the third *Iambus*, the cult of the Muses with the cult of orgiastic deities such as Adonis and Cybele (Callimachus, fr. 193.34ff, Pf.) although the images he conjures up are not quite as gruesome. He mentions the sound of the Phrygian flute which accompanies their ecstatic dance.

Throughout the third *Iambus*, Callimachus complains about his poverty. As a penniless poet, he cannot fulfil his sexual desires as easily as his rich rivals.[1] In a world that places material assets higher than spiritual values, it might be just as well to live as a eunuch-priest of Cybele or to be one of the women who lament the death of Adonis. To Callimachus, this fantasy suggests an antithesis of two ways of life, the Hellenic cult of the Muses, the daughters of Memory, and companions of Apollo – and the oriental cult of the senses, symbolized in the orgiastic ritual of Cybele and Adonis. The tragic fate of a Greek youth who has abandoned the first in order to embrace the second, is the theme of Catullus' 63rd poem, probably modelled after a Callimachean original.

When Priapus has ended his speech, Tibullus feels at once very confident. He already sees himself in the role of the *praeceptor amoris*, the 'teacher of love', and anticipates many appreciative and grateful pupils.

In an elegy from which Lucian quotes three lines (*Amores* 49 = Callimachus, fr. 571, Pf.), Callimachus had introduced a curious character, a certain Erchius, who poses as a specialist in the art of παιδοφιλεῖν, 'being a lover of boys'. The poet turns to those 'who look at youths with lecherous eyes' and urges them to follow Erchius' advice.

The motif is the same as in Tibullus, and so is the context. Priapus has taken, as it were, the role of Erchius. But the note of

---

[1] See my paper 'Kids and Wolves', *Class. Quart.* 1959, 34ff.

lechery that is inseparable from Priapus' character disappears as soon as Tibullus takes over his role. He does not intend to assist the sophisticated *roué*, but he wants to comfort those who suffer from unrequited love –

> . . . *me qui spernentur, amantes*
> *consulent . . .*
>
> (77-78)

Botle Propertius and Ovid are 'teachers of love' in this sense.

Tibullus' consciousness of his mission grows even stronger toward the end. He has a vision of himself as an old man, surrounded by an eager crowd of disciples, listening to his advice, while they escort him back to his house (79-80):

> *tempus erit, cum me Veneris praecepta ferentem*
> *deducat iuvenum sedula turba senem.*

Anacreon could have described himself in these terms, and the gaiety and exuberance of these lines does, indeed, recall the mood of archaic Greek lyrics. It seems, however, that they are modelled after some lines of Callimachus. In the first Book of the *Aitia* (fr. 41, Pf.), the Alexandrian poet pictured an old man who 'ages painlessly' and whom the young men love and, like a father, lead by the hand to his door:

> γηράσκει δ' ὁ γέρων κεῖνος ἐλαφρότερον,
> κοῦροι τὸν φιλέουσιν, ἑὸν δέ μιν οἷα γονῆα
> χειρὸς ἐπ' οἰκείην ἄχρις ἄγουσι θύρην.

What is told as part of a legend in Callimachus has been transformed into a personal ambition by the Roman poet. He identifies himself with the mythological character. The situation is the same, but the story is now more than a mere precedent. When Callimachus tells it, we feel that he is personally involved; he *likes* the old man. Tibullus has gone a step further; he *is* the old man.

But all his self-confidence vanishes as soon as he realizes how strong his love for Marathus is. What are all these precepts and devices in the face of the 'slow fire' that tortures him? He can only hope that Marathus will not be too unkind:

parce, puer, quaeso, ne turpis fabula fiam,
  cum mea ridebunt vana magisteria.

(83-84)

The poem ends on a note of self-irony. After having developed so confidently those *magisteria*, Tibullus suddenly denies them any value at all. Love is stronger than learning. In the last four lines, Tibullus has given back the elegy its personal character. Similarly, Callimachus, in his fifth *Iambus*, after a series of playfully veiled erotic allusions, suddenly turns to his beloved:

ἆ, μή με ποιήσῃς γέλω

'please don't make a fool of me.'

(Callimachus, fr. 195.30, Pf.)

This is more direct and more colloquial than Tibullus. But the situation is the same; it reflects the ἀμηχανία, the helplessness of the lover; the weakness of *ratio* in the presence of an irrational drive. Only the touch of romantic irony is new in Tibullus, an irony of which we find little evidence outside of the Marathus-cycle.

These 'Alexandrian' elegies do not seem to justify the traditional image of Tibullus as an idyllic and sentimental poet. They are urbane, a little self-conscious, and very carefully wrought. They also have the character of a literary experiment. On the other hand, only Tibullus could have written them, and they certainly reflect the taste and the interests of Messalla's circle with its special kind of sophistication.

6

Minor Talents

This survey of the Roman love-elegy should include not only the important names but also the lesser ones. Their works supply a sort of atmosphere to the poets one likes to know about. What fills out a tradition is mainly the bulk of lesser genius. The very word tradition implies a continuity, and therefore calls for disciples, imitators and followers to make a living chain.

In the *Corpus Tibullianum* we find not only the poems of Tibullus himself but also those of certain writers whose personalities are more or less in the dark. Tibullus is the author of Books I and II. A man who calls himself Lygdamus composed six elegies, now generally grouped together as Book III. There follows an anonymous panegyric on Messalla, in hexameters. A Roman lady, Sulpicia, is also represented, with six short erotic elegies. Someone else, fascinated by her romance, adapted her themes and situations in a cycle of five poems. Finally, there are two short elegies, possibly early works of Tibullus.

At one time (but when? and by whom?) these various collections were edited in one volume. Ever since, they have constituted a whole in the manuscript tradition. Its individual parts are of unequal literary value, but taken as a whole, they give a suggestive cross-section of Roman poetry and life during a relatively short period of time.

Most of the persons whose names occur in the *Corpus Tibullianum* are in some way or other connected with the house of Messalla Corvinus, the soldier, orator, statesman and patron of letters who was consul with Octavian in 31 B.C., the year of Actium. Tibullus was his companion-in-arms and close friend; Sulpicia was his ward; and the author of the panegyric was almost certainly one of his clients. Another friend or relative of his may be hiding behind the pseudonym 'Lygdamus'.

As a member of one of the oldest and most distinguished Roman families, Messalla[1] needed a historiographer of his military achievements. Since the days of the younger Scipio, it had become fashionable for a Roman *grand seigneur* to surround himself with poets, philosophers, artists. Augustus himself enrolled the greatest poets of his time as heralds of his political and cultural programme. It is only natural that Messalla, too, encouraged a writer to commemorate his exploits in the heroic manner. He had to content himself with a more modest talent; the author of the panegyric is no Horace or Vergil.

When this obscure versifier failed so miserably, Messalla must have realized that no laurels grew for him in this province of letters. It is interesting to see that his main influence turned in a completely different direction. His house became a centre of erotic poetry in Rome.

In the young Tibullus he found a promising representative of the love-elegy. In the meantime, Maecenas, too, had discovered an elegist – Propertius. Under these circumstances it must have been Messalla's ambition to fill the place that had become vacant through Tibullus' premature death, in order to restore his circle's special claim to distinction. He may have kept his eye on Ovid. Indeed, we know that Messalla encouraged Ovid as a very young man to publish his first poems.[2] One of them is *Amores* 3.9, on Tibullus' death.

But Ovid's earlier poetry shows nothing of Tibullus' devotion to Messalla. He must have emancipated himself quite early from Messalla's house. His private fortune and his rapid recognition made him independent. A few years after Tibullus' death Messalla's circle consisted only of more or less gifted dilettanti.

The youth of every generation writes the same kind of poetry.

---

[1] The following outline of Messalla's role in the development of the Latin elegy is based on an informative paper by R. Hanslik: *Anz. Oesterr. Ak. Wiss.*, *Phil.-Hist. Kl.* 89 (1952), 25 and 37f.

[2] Ovid, *Epistulae ex Ponto* 2.3.75ff, addressed to Messalla's younger son: *me tuus ille pater . . . primus ut auderem committere carmina famae impulit : ingenii dux fuit ille mei*, cf. *Epistulae ex Ponto* 1.7.27f; W. Kraus, RE 18.1914; R. Hanslik, RE 8A.136f; *Tristia* 4.4 is probably addressed to Messallinus, Messalla's elder son (Kraus, ibid. 1964; Lunzer, RE 8A.162); it contains similar praises (vv. 27ff).

Then, little by little, those few who are fated to do so find their originality, their special note or vision, the thing that they, and they alone can do. A secret door seems to open for them into a realm of the imagination which is theirs alone.

It is generally assumed that the *Corpus Tibullianum* was published from Messalla's 'archives', as a kind of document or memoir; the bad and the mediocre together with the good.[1] This edition must have been made at a time when there was still some interest in Messalla and his circle – although Messalla himself and his protégés may have been dead. For there is so much frankness in the verse of Lygdamus and Sulpicia that it might have been embarrassing to have them published during their lifetime. Their contemporaries knew who was hiding behind the pseudonyms, and, as a lady of high Roman society, Sulpicia was not as free as Sappho or Nossis.

The author of the six elegies which follow in the manuscripts after Tibullus' Book II[2] mentions his name just once:

> *Lygdamus hic situs est: dolor huic et cura Neaerae,*
> *coniugis ereptae, causa perire fuit.*

'Lygdamus lies here; his grief and love for Neaera, his mistress who had been taken away from him, were the cause of his death,'

(Lygdamus 2.29-30)

in a fictitious epitaph, a sentimental motif dear to the elegiac poets.

Who was Lygdamus? His name has been variously explained. The Greek λύγδος is 'white marble', and the adjective λύγδινος means 'marble-white', 'luminous'. Lygdamos could be a Greek translation of the Latin names Albius or Lucius. Another derivation, from the Greek λύγδην, suggests the tears and sighs that are so characteristic of this poet.

These etymologies are more or less playful (and quite inconclusive). It is easier to say who Lygdamus was not than to determine who he was.

---

[1] This theory has first been presented by C. Lachmann, in *Kl. Schriften* II 150ff.

[2] The discovery that Lygdamus cannot be identical with Tibullus on chronological grounds is due to J. H. Voss, the translator of Homer (*Musenalmanach für 1786*, 81 n.).

Lygdamus is not Tibullus. He says he was born in 43 B.C., about ten years after Tibullus.

> *natalem primo nostrum videre parentes,*
> *cum cecidit fato consul uterque pari.*

'My parents saw my birthday for the first time, when both consuls were killed by the same destiny.'

(Lygdamus 5.17-18)

This is the year of the battle of Mutina, in the war against Antony, during which Hirtius and Pansa, the two consuls of the year, were both killed. It is also the year in which Ovid was born. Strangely enough Ovid refers to it in the very same words (*Tristia* 4.10.6).

But Lygdamus is not Ovid, either. Their poetic personalities are totally different. In his earliest poems Ovid shows a mind and a style of his own. It is probable that the two men knew each other in Messalla's house and that they read each other's poems, but they are certainly not one and the same person.

As to that curious line – it is used by Lygdamus when he is still *iuvenis* (Lygdamus 5.6, cf. v. 15f), that is, before the age of thirty-five; but Ovid is over fifty when the same line occurs to him. Is he quoting Lygdamus? Or are both poets quoting a third one? We cannot possibly deal with all the attempts that have been made to identify Lygdamus. There are too many candidates among the crowd of poets and would-be poets who were active in Rome at this time.[1]

The evidence of the poems themselves is a little more concrete than these speculations. Lygdamus was by no means a Greek slave or freedman, as his pseudonym seems to suggest. Like Propertius' friends 'Lynceus' and 'Demophoon' he belongs to a noble Roman family, otherwise he would hardly have been accepted into Messalla's aristocratic circle. Maecenas was more democratic in his choice of poets; he paid no attention to the fact that Horace was the son of a freedman, but Messalla's protégés were all of noble birth.

Lygdamus makes this plain in the first distich of his booklet.

---

[1] There is also some metrical evidence against Lygdamus' being either Ovid or Tibullus; F. H. Sandbach, *Class. Rev.* (1949), 106; M. Platnauer, *Latin Elegiac Verse* (1951), 38, 47, 64.

He expects to be buried in a marble sarcophagus (Lygdamus 2.21f). Neaera, his mistress, is a Roman lady from a *culta domus*, a 'refined (or cultured) house' (Lygdamus 4.92); and when she falls in love with a plebeian he freezes with indignation (Lygdamus 6.59f).

Whoever he was, he was no great poet. He has talent and is well read but lacks creative boldness; he does not have the urge to experiment and remains, in short, the eternal dilettante. We miss in his verse the variety of themes and moods that make Tibullus and Propertius so abundantly alive. Lygdamus has only one theme: 'I love and am not loved; I want to die.'

The lyrical confession of his love is interrupted here and there by vague biographical references. It seems that at one time he lived happily with Neaera. 'Once your husband (*vir*), now your brother', he calls himself (Lygdamus 1.23). This does not mean that they were actually married. The terms *vir* or *coniunx*, 'man' and 'wife', have no well-defined meaning in Latin love-poetry. They sometimes suggest a legal, always a sentimental relationship. Later they were separated; someone 'took her away' from him (Lygdamus 2.1ff, cf. v.30).

The first poem introduces the name of his mistress, Neaera (in v.6), to whom the whole booklet is dedicated. The handsome scroll, an *édition de luxe*, is described in a manner that shows the influence of Catullus' references to his *lepidus libellus*. Its title, visible on the outside, is simply NEAERA (Lygdamus 1.9-14).[1] This scroll comes to Neaera as a gift from the poet on the *Matronalia*, a festival in honour of Juno on the first of March.

The following five elegies (perhaps selected by the editor of the *Corpus Tibullianum* from a larger number) present the various stages of his estrangement. They are all pervaded by a sense that something the poet has been longing and waiting for had slipped his grasp just as it had come within reach. No strict chronological order can be detected, unless one stresses the function of

[1] The author calls it *comptum opus*, 'a neat piece of work' – surely a Catullan reminiscence. On the technical side of his description see Ellis' notes on Catullus c. 22.7f. The emphasis is on bright colours, on exquisite craftsmanship. Ovid's introduction to his first book of the *Tristia* (1.1.5ff) suggests the very opposite. The *titulus index* attached to Lygdamus' scroll probably had NEAERA without the name of the author (it occurs in the second elegy). CYNTHIA seems to have been the title of Propertius' first book of elegies (cf. 2.24.2); it is the first word of the first poem.

the first poem as a prologue and argues that it was the last to be composed.

Most of his themes have become conventional by that time, and he does little to give them an individual note. Like Tibullus, he is haunted by a premonition of his early death; and like Propertius, he describes the vision of his own funeral with mournful delight (2.9ff.).[1] It is difficult to present these sentimental and slightly outworn themes in a new light.

Once he is dangerously ill. He knows that Neaera is enjoying the 'purple spring' in a fashionable resort while he is struggling in the 'black hour' of death. This antithesis – suggested here, as often in Lygdamus, by a contrast of colours – goes throughout a whole poem (5.3f, 15, 33f).

Another theme, probably borrowed from Tibullus, is the contempt of wealth: 'I do not care for a kingdom, nor for the gold of the Lydian river, nor for all the riches produced in all the earth. Let others crave for this; may it be my privilege to enjoy, in poverty, the safe presence of my dear girl' (3.29-32).[2] All this is a little rhetorical and not too convincing. Still, it is remarkable that even such a snob as Lygdamus can work up a certain amount of enthusiasm when he praises poverty.

The elegy which is, perhaps, most characteristic for Lygdamus' manner is the fourth. Presumably we have here the earliest work of the cycle, because it suggests the beginning of the estrangement between himself and Neaera. Its theme is the inevitable arrival of disillusionment.

It consists mainly of set pieces or purple passages rather loosely strung together. There is, for example, a memorable description of night and sleep (in vv. 19-22), a very decorative passage, but too 'literary' in the bad sense of the word. There is a charming mythological digression – the god Apollo in love, vv. 67-72 – but it is recited in the solemn tone of a classroom declamation. Passages from Catullus[3] are adapted more or less skilfully throughout the poem.

[1] Cf. Propertius 2.13.17ff. G. Rohde, s.v. *ossilegium*, RE 18.1599f, provides a valuable commentary on Lygdamus' lines.

[2] Cf. Tibullus 1.1.1ff, Catullus 45.21ff.

[3] There is an obvious quotation from Catullus 64.154ff in vv. 89ff (cf. 6.41f, where he seems to acknowledge his debt); cf. also 29ff and Catullus 61.191ff, 35 and Catullus 64.308 (Prop. 3.17.32; Verg. *Aen.* 1.404); also 52 and Catullus 70.3

All this betrays a youthful poet's literary self-consciousness. Lygdamus assumes various airs and graces and is inclined to watch his own effects. In the manner of the *poetae novi*, he sprinkles his poetry liberally with clever parallels, exquisite reminders that would delight the informed reader.

But it is always a conventional concept that is dressed up in some striking new clothes, the new clothes being the real *raison d'être*. The whole machinery of rhetorical devices, the stage-properties of the dilettante, are somewhat tedious. Yet there is a great deal of charm in Lygdamus' attempt to conjure up these sweet words, and the clouds of his nostalgia lend to his verse a certain melancholy distinction.

How much do we really know about the women of the elegiac poets? In Tibullus' verse Delia and Nemesis never emerge very clearly from the romantic mist that surrounds them. Ovid's Corinna is a composite figure, only half real and half the product of his day-dreams and literary reminiscences. Catullus' portrait of Lesbia is to us more strikingly realistic, but mainly because we interpret it in terms of contemporary reports on her character and life.

Which one is the real Lesbia – the woman to whom Catullus addressed his lyrics, or the woman whom Cicero describes with heavy sarcasm?[1] Was Cynthia that lovely and refined girl whom Propertius worships in his tender moods, or was she that selfish, promiscuous creature that he pursues with bitter invectives?

The question, asked in this form, must remain unanswered. A poem is not a biographical or sociological document. The image born of images, the world abstracted from abstractions, is no longer related to actuality. It is easy to write down generalities, to say, for example, that the high status of the woman in Roman society was one of the main reasons or conditions for the rapid growth of a new kind of love-poetry. It is more difficult to define the particular fascination of these particular women.

For one thing, they were cultured. Propertius claims that it

(combined with 78.4), 93 and Catullus 68.159. The relationship between Catullus and Lygdamus would justify a separate study.

[1] In his speech *Pro Caelio*, and elsewhere. If we believe Cicero, she was a notorious nymphomaniac; she poisoned her husband and had incestuous relations with her brother.

was Cynthia's *doctrina*, her literary and artistic achievements, that he really admired. She writes poetry herself (1.2.27). She sings and recites poetry, including Propertius' own, to the accompaniment of the lyre (1.3.42, 2.1.9f, 2.26.25). Thanks to her good taste, she is a wonderful audience (2.13.11f, 2.24B.21). He has a vision of her dancing as the tenth Muse among the nine others, a compliment usually reserved to Sappho (2.30.37-40). By a similar association, a Ptolemaic Queen appears as the fourth Charis in one of Callimachus' epigrams (51, Pf.).

Cynthia's verses have perished, but those of another *puella docta* are preserved in the *Corpus Tibullianum*. There are six short elegies forming a cycle. Each one is clearly written by a woman who introduces herself in the fourth poem as

> *Servi filia Sulpicia,*
>
> 'Sulpicia, daughter of Servius.'
> (Sulpicia 4.4 = 'Tibullus' 3.16.4)

She is the daughter of Servius Sulpicius Rufus; she is also a niece and, after her father's death, the ward of Messalla. At the time when these poems were written she was in love with a man named Cerinthus, of whom we know nothing.[1]

The longest of these poems has ten lines, the shortest four. They all have the character of letters, *billets doux*, with vivid apostrophes and questions. Written spontaneously by a woman with no literary pretensions, they are a unique document in the history of Latin literature.

Sulpicia's poetry does not convey a romantic distillation of life, but life itself speaks forth from these lines, directly, often carelessly, but always believably. If they are judged by the high standards that Catullus and the *poetae novi* had established, they suggest a regression in technique. But as the record of the private life of a Roman lady, they are remarkable. They show that, in Messalla's circle, even *poésies d'occasion*, written by an amateur under the impact of a strong emotion, had reached a surprisingly high level. In any event, they are the background against which we should judge the performance of Tibullus.

---

[1] The speculations of Richard Bentley (in his note on Horace, *Sat.* 1.2.81) on the identity of Cerinthus are ingenious, but hardly conclusive.

The first and the last poem correspond to each other. In the last, Sulpicia knows that Cerinthus is in love with her, but she hesitates to reveal her own passion (Sulpicia 6.6 = 'Tibullus' 3.18.6). In the first, however, she has thrown overboard all conventions. She is proud of her love; she wants everybody to know about it:

> sed peccasse iuvat, vultus componere famae
> taedet: cum digno digna fuisse ferar.

'But I am glad to have "sinned", it is tiresome to set up a face for the sake of reputation; let it be known that I have been worthy of a lover worthy of me.'[1]

(Sulpicia 1.9-10 = 'Tibullus' 3.13.9-10)

Sulpicia's verse-epistles are by no means great poetry. She has the reputation of a *puella docta* in Messalla's circle ('Tibullus' 3.12.2), but she moves in a limited world of images. In her forty lines there is not a single mythological allusion. This observation by itself proves nothing about the literary value of her work, but it shows that she is unable or, perhaps, unwilling to look at the persons and events of her world from a distance.

There is the city – 'what is more pleasant than the city?' (Sulpicia 2.3) – and the country, where, unlike Tibullus, she does not feel at home. There is Cerinthus, her lover (she calls him *mea lux*, 'my life' or *meus*, 'my man'), there is a *scortum*, a low-class woman to whom Cerinthus seems to be attracted at one time, and there is Messalla, her guardian, watchful and a little suspicious. There are the gods – but only Venus and the Muses are mentioned.

Sulpicia deals in her poems with the simple events of a woman's life: her birthday, an illness, a trip, the day she knows what love means.

All this is told in simple outlines, with none of the preciosity and studied elegance of Lygdamus. The language of Sulpicia is straightforward, sometimes harsh, with a tendency toward the colloquial. Philologists have labelled it, not very politely, 'ladies' Latin'.

---

[1] 'To be with someone' is an euphemism of the *sermo amatorius*, cf. Ovid, *Amores* 2.8.27f, threatening Corinna's maid: 'I shall tell your mistress where I have been with you (*tecum fuerim*), and how many times, and how often, and in what ways.'

Anyone who thinks Propertius morbid and Tibullus a dreamer will find Sulpicia refreshing. There is something wholesome about her view of life. She knows what she likes and dislikes. Occasionally her strong beliefs are put in a somewhat naïve form. For Sulpicia, things are either nice or unpleasant. The city is a nice place, the country is an unpleasant place (*molestum*); love is a nice thing (*mea gaudia*), illness is an unpleasant thing (*tristes morbos*).

Sulpicia is no Roman Sappho or Erinna, and her craftsmanship cannot be compared to that of Nossis or Anyte, whose epigrams always have a professional touch. If Sulpicia's poems have been preserved, it is not for the sake of their literary merit, but because of Messalla's natural interest in the poetical experiments of his niece . . . and because they are the point of departure for another cycle of elegies, composed by a more talented member of the circle. This is the author of *Corp. Tibull.* 3.8-12.

Throughout the history of the ancient elegy, the same general themes occur again and again, treated differently by different poets. There are commonplaces on love, beauty and parting that appear, with individual variations, from Mimnermus to Ovid. The more concrete and specific a theme is, the less it lends itself to imitation or adaptation. *Omnia vincit Amor*, 'Love conquers all' – this is a general theme; but 'Sulpicia is in love with Cerinthus' reflects a specific situation. It is a singular case in ancient poetry that such an individual theme, the love of two individuals, two contemporaries, has been treated by two different poets.

For Sulpicia, this love is her own personal experience. For the anonymous poet of Messalla's circle, it becomes a little drama that he watches from a close distance with sympathy and fascination. He resumes most of Sulpicia's themes and expands them in five elegies, as though he wanted to show her how it could have been done. He adds two motifs of his own; a description of Sulpicia's beauty in the first; and a diatribe against hunting in the second elegy. In these five poems he speaks either as a kind of ideal spectator, like the chorus in a Greek drama (the first, third and fifth poem), or he identifies himself with Sulpicia, interpreting and decorating her feelings and moods as he knew them from her own collection of verse (the second and fourth poems).

We should like to know who this poet was. Unlike Lygdamus and Sulpicia, he never names himself. Was he Tibullus? But

Tibullus' art is less rational; he is more of a lyric poet, the unknown author more of a dramatist.

These five poems take a position apart in the history of the Latin love-elegy. Although they are influenced by the work of Tibullus and Propertius, they represent an earlier type of the elegy. They are closer to the mythological love-poems of the Alexandrians. The heroes and heroines of the legend have been replaced by two contemporary characters – one step forward in the direction of the subjective love-elegy of Tibullus and Propertius. The protagonist, Sulpicia, is introduced by her real name; her lover is known only by a Greek pseudonym. He takes the place of Lesbia, Cynthia, Delia, whose real names were no secret at the time, although they are not revealed by the poet himself.

What is different and, as far as we can see, quite singular, is the fact that the author does not speak of his personal experience and, at the same time, does not identify himself completely with someone else. In two poems he is Sulpicia, but in the remaining three, he is just a sympathetic observer. This shifting point of view is the result of an artistic intention, not the symptom of immaturity or indecision. The conscious arrangement ($1/3/5$ and $2/4$) shows that the poet aims at a new effect.

The closest parallels to this technique are found in Propertius. One is the letter of Arethusa to Lycotas (Propertius 4.3). A Roman lady and her soldier-husband are hiding under these heroic names. The poem is a dramatic monologue, in the form of an epistle, written by Arethusa. The poet, Propertius, remains in the background. This is also the situation of Ovid's *Heroides*.

The other example is Propertius 3.12, *Postume, plorantem potuisti linquere Gallam . . .?* 'Postumus, you could leave Galla in tears . . .?' This is not a letter, but a monologue, delivered by the poet, Propertius himself, *on behalf of* Aelia Galla. The situation is the same; a Roman knight (this time known by his real name) has to say goodbye to his wife to 'follow the brave standards of Augustus'. The poet assumes the role of a friend and does not identify himself with the woman.

These two elegies of Propertius are 'objective' in the sense that the poet never speaks of his own love. Both are relatively late works, the second published around 22 B.C., the first shortly before 16 B.C. In the whole of Propertius' work they have the character of occasional poems. Their theme, their mood, and their pathos, are the same.

The anonymous author *de Sulpicia* has learnt a great deal from Propertius.[1] He has realized the dramatic possibilities of this form of composition and adopted it consistently throughout a short series of poems.

His vocabulary is not that of Tibullus. Only about three-quarters of the words he uses are found in Tibullus' two books of verse. The technical character of the hunting-poem (*Corp. Tibull.* 3.9) reduces the value of these statistics; it is evident, nevertheless, that in many cases Tibullus prefers another word for the same idea.[2] Other stylistic features – such as the use of the elative superlative, which is strictly avoided by Tibullus – further distinguish the manner of the unknown poet.

We find in his work parallels to the later works of Propertius which were published after Tibullus' death. There are also a few distant reminiscences of Ovid's earlier works, but no allusions, as far as we can see, to the poems which Ovid wrote in exile.[3] Since Ovid was banished in A.D. 8, the year of Messalla's death, this may be the date when the collection was ready for publication.

If these chronological conclusions are valid, we have here a poet who followed from a distance the trends of elegiac love-poetry. For some reason he cannot make Sulpicia the heroine of his collection. In the meantime Ovid had revived the objective mythological elegy of the Alexandrians in a new form, the love-letter. This is the medium which our poet adopts.

Thus it seems very unlikely that he is identical with the young Ovid who belonged, for a while, to Messalla's circle and was encouraged by Messalla himself to publish his verse. The objective style of the *Heroides* represents a later phase in the development of

---

[1] This poet is as close to Propertius in his manner of writing as Lygdamus is to Catullus. His first elegy is full of reminiscences from the 'Roman Callimachus'. As the elegy established itself in Roman literature, its Roman representatives rose to the status of their Greek models and became the models of the second or third generation of elegiac poets and would-be poets.

[2] There is a careful study of the vocabulary of the 'Garland', by R. Zimmermann, *Philologus* (1928), 400ff.

[3] Cf. Zimmermann, 413; H. Fuchs, *Erasmus* (1947), 341f.

Ovid but is not necessarily a symptom of the exhaustion of the traditional form of the love-elegy.[1]

This anonymous poet whom we might call *amicus Sulpiciae*, 'friend of Sulpicia', was simply another dilettante who had educated his sensibility and polished his style by reading the masters. He is attractive and cultured, more talented, less precious than Lygdamus. His introductory poem reminds one of Lygdamus' first elegy. The title of the booklet, SULPICIA, is indicated in the first distich, because the name fits conveniently into the elegiac metre. Lygdamus' description of the booklet is replaced by a description of Sulpicia herself.

The occasion is the same. On the first of March, the *Matronalia*, Sulpicia receives these poems as a gift. It seems that on this day presents were sent only to married ladies and by none but married men. This throws a curious light on the poetry that was cultivated in Messalla's house. With the exception of Tibullus' and Sulpicia's verse, these are primarily *vers de société*, written with a smile, intended to decorate special occasions, birthdays and anniversaries.

What the *amicus Sulpiciae* has written is literature as a means of refined and intellectual pleasure, to be enjoyed by persons of sufficient leisure and breeding. His verses are not dictated by an inner conflict. In every poem he deals with a neatly circumscribed artistic problem and solves it in the manner of a good craftsman.

The first poem with its numerous reminiscences from Propertius is like a compliment to one of the masters of the love-elegy. The technique of the composition is that of Propertius. Yet the whole does not seem to be pieced together; it is fresh and direct; the traditional motives fall into place, and there is not a word too much.

The second poem is more original. Its theme is related to that of Euripides' *Hippolytus*. Cerinthus goes hunting and leaves Sulpicia alone. This is one pleasure she cannot share with him;

[1] Two papyri (one of them written in the first century B.C.) contain fragments of a novel in epistolary form, relating to the life of Alexander the Great, blending fact and fiction. R. Merkelbach, *Die Quellen des griechischen Alexanderromans* (*Zetemata* 9, 1954), has shown that the anonymous author is primarily interested in Alexander's character. This type of 'light reading' (Merkelbach, p. 33) provides, in a sense, a parallel to Ovid's *Heroides*. Its technique of psychological portraiture is that of Hellenistic rhetoric.

convention bids her to stay at home, but how she would like to accompany him through the woods, and across the fields! An unexpected twist – but the phrasing is suggested by the famous outcry of the Euripidean Phaedra:

> 'Bring me to the mountains! I will go to the forest
> Among the pine trees where the dogs tread
> that kill wild beasts,
> Hanging upon the heels of the spotted stags. . . .'
>
> (Euripides, *Hippolytus*, vv. 215ff)[1]

The following poem (3.10) is a variation of the ὕμνος κλητικός, the 'invocatory hymn', a traditional prayer in distress. Sulpicia is sick and Apollo, as the healing god, is urged to bring her relief and restore her to good health. The same theme had been treated by Propertius and Ovid.[2]

Two birthday poems, one for Cerinthus and one for Sulpicia, conclude the series. Although they are both rather conventional, I should like to point out the very unusual mode of composition represented by the former.

If one reads this elegy (*Corp. Tibull.* 3.11) several times, one notices a kind of *progression d'effet* by which the central idea of each distich is regularly repeated and developed in the following one. To show this in detail would require a long analysis; it may be sufficient to say that the principle is most obvious in vv. 6-7 and 8-9, where the very words, not only the ideas, are repeated. The end of the poem leads back to the beginning, thus forming a closed chain of ideas and images. It is all a little too calculated to be more than an intellectual entertainment, but it shows how

[1] Translated by David Grene (Univ. of Chicago Press 1942).

[2] Cf. Propertius 2.28 (A and B); Ovid, *Amores* 2.13 and 14. On their relationship to Pseudo-Tibullus, see R. Bürger, *Hermes* (1905), 330; R. Neumann, *Qua ratione Ovidius in amoribus scribendis Propertii elegiis usus sit* (Diss. Gött. 1919), 54-59. Propertius addresses his prayer to Jupiter Opitulus (= Zeus Soter), Ovid to Isis (Ilithyia, cf. Diana, Propertius v. 60). Certain motifs are common to Propertius and Pseudo-Tibullus (e.g. the girl deserves divine help because she is so beautiful, Propertius v. 2 and Pseudo-Tibullus v. 3f; Ovid 2.13.22 says merely that Corinna is 'worthy'; she will render thanks to the gods, Propertius v. 59f and Pseudo-Tibullus v. 23f; Ovid will do this himself, 2.13.23ff). Other motifs are common to Propertius and Ovid (e.g. Propertius 45 and Ovid 2.13.17; Propertius 43f and Ovid 25). One very characteristic theme is common to all three poems: the gods, saving one, will save both (Propertius 41f, Ovid 15; Pseudo-Tibullus 19f).

much Messalla's circle enjoyed technical experiments, the knowing twists of an art that had become primarily a civilized pastime.

Compared to Tibullus and Propertius the *amicus Sulpiciae* is a minor poet. His is indeed a poetry which aims at a smooth, elegant presentation; and for many readers this may have been perfectly satisfying. His verse never approaches the complex themes of an excited consciousness; his imagery remains subdued, conventional. But he is an endearing figure, because he is able to write with such genuine enthusiasm about someone else's love; and his understanding of the woman's soul is as sensitive as that of Euripides and Ovid. His five short elegies are polished accounts of typical human situations, decorative, graceful and a little sentimental.

At the very end of the *Corpus Tibullianum* there are two more love-poems, one, an elegy of twenty-four lines; the other, an elegiac quatrain (3.19 and 20). The author of the former names himself in v. 13 as 'Tibullus'. He may be identical with the author of the latter because of the similarities in theme and style. There is some doubt today that both are genuine works of the young Tibullus.[1]

During this early phase he must have been, like Lygdamus, under the influence of the *poetae novi*. Themes, language and style remind one of Catullus and his Hellenistic models. The concept of love as a *foedus aeternum*, an 'eternal union',[2] the emphasis on the subjective appreciation of beauty,[3] the formula *tu mihi sola places*, 'you alone appeal to me',[4] the simplicity and intensity of feeling – all this seems part of the neoteric heritage.

But the young Tibullus is already an accomplished craftsman; this can be shown by a study of the verse-technique and sentence-

[1] For their authenticity, see F. Lenz, *Studi Ital. di Filol. Class.* (1932/3), 125-145; U. Knoche, *Navicula Chiloniensis* (Studies in Honour of F. Jacoby, 1956), 173ff, in an ingenious paper, has denied it – without giving a good reason why a forger should have used Tibullus' name (v. 13).

[2] V. 2, cf. Catullus 109.6; R. Reitzenstein, *Sitzungsber. Heidelberg* (1912), nr. 19, pp. 9ff; E. Burck, *Hermes* (1952), 168f. E. Paratore, *Aevum* (1949), 94, takes a slightly different point of view; he thinks that the concept of the 'eternal union' is not typically Roman, but rather Hellenistic (Antimachus, Philetas, Parthenius, and their elegies dedicated to a mistress or wife).

[3] Cf. Callimachus, *Ep.* 29.3f (Pf.); Catullus c. 86; Meleager, *Anth. Pal.* 12.60 and 106.　　　　[4] Cf. Propertius 1.11.23, 2.7.19f; Ovid, *Ars. Am.* 1.42.

structure. In the first distich of the first elegy, each line is formed by a complete sentence. In the second distich, there is a short, but significant sentence – *tu mihi sola places* – which takes up the first half of the hexameter and is followed by a long sentence which fills the rest of the distich. The weight of the sentences increases progressively.

A third variety of metrical structure is represented by the third distich; the hexameter has the form of an exclamation, while the two parts of the pentameter are filled with a wish and the result of its fulfilment. In the fourth distich this procedure is reversed. The reader has the impression that he has reached a resting point.

The fifth distich is, again, built according to the same principle as the first. Two long sentences take up a single line each. The sixth distich represents a variation of the metrical structure of the second. It consists of clauses of unequal length, whereby the longest stands at the end. This arrangement, which is emphasized by the repetition of *tu*, gives the impression that one clause is crowding or chasing the other, as if each incantation must be followed by a more significant one.

The seventh distich repeats the metrical structure of the third – one sentence in the hexameter, two shorter co-ordinate clauses filling the two halves of the pentameter. Here the symmetry ends. It might have become monotonous, and a poem should not be a mathematical equation. The eighth distich reflects once more the quiet tone of the first and fifth and marks the end of the first part of the elegy.

The two main themes of this first part are these: 'I think you are beautiful, but I am afraid that too many men in this city think so too', and 'You are everything I have in the world.' The former is a variation of a popular Hellenistic theme, the latter a motif famous in ancient poetry since Homer.[1]

A lesser poet than Tibullus would have ended the poem at this point, but he wants to break through the literary conventions.

---

[1] *Iliad* 6.429f (Andromache to Hector), 'you are father to me, and my honoured mother, / you are my brother, and you it is who are my young husband' (Transl. R. Lattimore, Univ. of Chicago Press 1951). In Latin love-poetry this relationship between man and woman is often reversed, e.g. Catullus 72.3f, Propertius 1.11.23f; cf. F. Klingner, in *Entretiens sur l'antiquité classique*, published by the *Fondation Hardt*, vol. II (1953), 212. O. Weinreich, *Die Distichen des Catull* (1926), 95, n. 5.

As soon as he has revealed his love, he seems to shrink back from his own frankness. He knows that he has given himself away (vv. 17-20). Does this afterthought damage the spontaneous feeling of the first part? No, on the contrary, it adds a new dimension to the main theme. Tibullus is willing to lose his freedom; but instead of taking this loss for granted, he lets the reader see how it happened, gradually, inevitably.

The last distich of the poem, as often in Tibullus, returns to the theme of the beginning, the idea of the *foedus aeternum*.

This is a lively poem, almost a little drama, with its range of shifting and fluctuating emotions – wish, exclamation, after-thought, remorse, cheerful acceptance.[1] On a small scale this is already the thematic development of the great elegies of Book I. It is the same longing for a love that would be pure, non-possessive and everlasting. The secrets of Tibullus' art are evident already in this early work, his delicate perception of shades of feeling and his unobtrusive technique.

The last poem of the *Corpus Tibullianum*, an epigram, recalls the directness and simplicity of Sulpicia's *billets doux*. Rumour tells him that his mistress is unfaithful. Instead of reproaching or accusing her, he simply wishes to be deaf. He knows that the rumour is right, but he chooses to ignore the facts.

The mood of this poem recalls Catullus' short elegies. The situation of the lover who is torn between suspicion and faith, hatred and love, is that of Catullus 85 and 76. But Catullus, in the famous distich *Odi et amo*, 'I love and I hate', simply states the dilemma, without any attempt at an explanation. And at the end of the moving elegy 76 he has given up hope that Lesbia might ever love him. His own fatal attachment appears to him as a *taeter morbus*, a 'dreadful disease'.

In Tibullus' early poem we find, for the first time in the history of the motif, the conscious effort of the lover to disregard reality. His love exists in a world all its own and cannot be measured by conventional standards. It is so strong that it absorbs the external world and transforms it into something new. In its quiet, un-pretentious way, this little poem has set forth an idealized con-

---

[1] This range of emotions seems more characteristic of Roman than of Greek love-poetry; cf. the epigram of Q. Lutatius Catulus (above, p. 40f) and its Greek 'original', Callimachus *Ep.* 41 (Pf.).

cept of love that is unknown to the Hellenistic epigram and the earlier Latin elegy.

Propertius has dealt with the same theme in a long, fairly elaborate poem (2.32). He touches on some of the same points, notably the question of *crimen*, and *rumor*. But Propertius, as usual, is more systematic; he distinguishes between minor and major 'crimes' and claims to consider the problem of Cynthia's reputation objectively, without any respect to his own person. In another elegy, however, he assures Cynthia that

> *de te quodcumque, ad surdas mihi dicitur auris*

'whatever is said to me about you meets deaf ears',
(Propertius 2.20.13)

but this promise occurs in a different context, for Propertius is anxious to defend himself against rumours that concern his person.

Propertius 2.32 served as a model to Ovid's superbly constructed poem *Amores* 3.14, which we shall discuss in a later chapter. It does not have the finality of Tibullus' epigram. In Ovid everything appears in a diffuse, shifting light. Tibullus' simple 'Yes' and 'No' has become an elaborate 'Perhaps'.

7

The Poet from Umbria

In his catalogue of the Latin elegiac poets, Ovid lists their names in 'chronological order' (*series temporis*). Tibullus succeeds Gallus and is succeeded in turn by Propertius. Ovid himself comes last (Ovid, *Tristia* 4.10.51ff; the same order is observed *Tristia* 2.445ff). If we press this statement, it must mean that Propertius was slightly older than Ovid himself, but a few years younger than Tibullus, who was born in 55 B.C. or later. Hence we can place the year of Propertius' birth between 55 and 43, let us say, around 50 B.C.

For all practical purposes Tibullus and Propertius were contemporaries and for this very reason presumably rivals. They never mention each other; they both have their friends and partisans. Horace, for example, addresses poems to Tibullus but never to Propertius; and Domitius Marsus, in or shortly after 19 B.C., completely overlooks Propertius when he declares that the Latin love-elegy died with Tibullus. Ovid, who is younger than both, can afford to be impartial; he hails both poets as his masters and gives them their due share of recognition.

Most of what we know about Propertius' life comes from his own poems. As a young man he had to introduce himself to his readers, to put his 'seal' (σφραγίς), as it were, on his first book. The result is a short poem (1.22), perhaps incomplete in our manuscripts, which tells us very little about the author. His youth has been overshadowed by the civil wars. The other themes of this poem – his friendship with Tullus, the loss of a close friend or relative on the battlefield – take up just as much space.

When Propertius published Book IV he was a famous writer and could expect more interest in biographical details. In the introductory poem to his last book he mentions his birthplace, adding that his genius will make it immortal. He was born in Umbria, near Perugia, and the foggy Mevania (Bevagna). His home town was probably Assisi (4.1.125, if we accept Lachmann's conjecture for MS. *Asis*), a small hill town. Inscriptions found in the vicinity record the name of the *gens Propertia*; even one of Propertius' descendants, C. Passennus Paullus, an elegiac poet himself, seems to have lived there at one time.

Propertius lost his father when he was still a boy (4.1.127f), assumed the toga of manhood in his mother's house and was faced with the choice of a career. Since his family was of equestrian rank, he was expected to go into law or politics. He became a poet and a 'Soldier of Venus' (4.1.137) instead. In Rome he had met other young men of good families (Tullus, Gallus, Ponticus) who were dabbling in literature. After the success of his first book of verse, Maecenas became interested in him; he met Vergil and moved into a house on the Esquiline. His personal relations with the Imperial House became closer over the years; in 22 B.C. he writes an elegy on the death of Marcellus, and a few years later he composes a dirge for Cornelia, the daughter of Scribonia by an earlier marriage.

His first poems, however, are love-poems. As a very young man he had an affair with a slave-girl, Lycinna, whom he remembers affectionately because of her unselfishness and her experience (3.15). But it was 'Cynthia', a Roman lady (her real name was Hostia) who made a poet of him:

> *non haec Calliope, non haec mihi cantat Apollo,*
> *ingenium nobis ipsa puella facit.*

'Neither Calliope nor Apollo dictates these poems to me; my lady herself is the cause of my genius.'[1]

(Propertius 2.1.3f)

---

[1] Cf. 2.30.40 *nam sine te nostrum non valet ingenium*; Ovid, *Amores* 3.12.16, 2.17.34, and later, in exile, *Tristia* 5.1.27f, *non haec ingenio, non haec componimus arte; materia est propriis ingeniosa malis*, doubtless a reminiscence of Propertius' passage.

Cynthia lives on in Propertius' poems, with all her qualities and defects, as a beautiful, cultured and reckless woman, capable of making him very happy and very miserable. At the beginning of this affair, he is wholly devoted to her; he writes later on, in retrospect:

cuncta tuus sepelivit amor,

'my love for you has buried everything.'

(Propertius 3.15.9)

The ups and downs, the joys and disenchantments of this romance are the fabric of most of his earlier poems. As the years go by, he feels attracted by other themes: he toys with the idea of writing an epic in honour of Augustus (Maecenas encourages him time and again to embark on this venture); later on (in Book III) he seems mainly concerned with his mission as a poet; he also writes funeral elegies and moral diatribes; and finally, in Book IV, he delves into Rome's past in his so-called 'Roman Elegies', conceived as companion-pieces to Callimachus' *Aitia*.

Unlike Tibullus, Propertius is a poet of the city. Unlike Catullus' poems, those of Propertius are not really poems of love, but poems about love, speculations on what it is, and exercises in new manners of celebrating it. This is particularly evident in Book I. His earliest elegies are not, as a rule, addressed directly to Cynthia, but to fellow-poets (Lynceus, Demophoon), as if they were entries in an endless contest in which the competitors and judges are the same, and the prize is 'fame', *gloria*.

The modern reader finds Propertius difficult because the progression of thought in his poems is often abrupt. He skims over details; his transitions are often harsh and forced; his repetitions bold, his images extravagant. This may be partly the result of an inadequate application of Alexandrian technique. He is unwilling to abandon the flamboyant and literary for the lucid and simple, but his ability to handle heavily ornamented lines is not as competent as that of Callimachus.

Propertius' choice of words and images is so daring that his context is often rather puzzling. He tries to say too much at the same time; he heaps allusion upon allusion and suddenly, involved in the difficulties he has created for himself, simply changes the subject. Should one attribute the many obscure passages in this author to 'poetic licence' or to the corrupt manuscript tradition? In many cases the scribes, not the poet, are to blame, and we must have the courage to accept plausible emendations.

Ever since J. J. Scaliger's important edition (Paris 1577), the traditional text has been changed over and over again in many places. Thousands of conjectures and transpositions of lines (or groups of lines) have accumulated over the years in the various editions since Scaliger. No modern editor could list them all. It has been suggested more recently that our text is full of interpolations. This would mean that we have to distinguish between the real Propertius and one or several imitators, who added or substituted whole new passages, either because they could not read what was originally there or because they thought it was not good enough. By this reasoning the field opens for the wildest speculations. *Quot editores, tot Propertii.*[1]

Propertius would have found congenial spirits in nineteenth-century Paris among the *Symbolistes*. More recently Ezra Pound has rediscovered him. There is something in the Umbrian poet that appeals to the modern mind, whether it is the rich texture of his imagery or rather his desire to avoid the banal and conventional at all costs.[2]

Propertius' 'difficulty', his 'obscurity' is to some extent doubtless intended. He could be as lucid as Ovid, if he chose, but he refuses to say the obvious and to say it over and over again, as Ovid occasionally did. Propertius wants to dazzle the reader; he wants to keep him guessing, to strike him by an unexpected remark or turn of phrase. Most of the time he moves on two levels, that of reality and that of imagination. If he had kept the two spheres apart, it would be easier to follow his train of thought; but as it is, he travels back and forth. As soon as he has outlined a real situation (for example in 1.3 the description of Cynthia asleep), he switches into mythological *exempla* and back to reality again with hardly any transition at all.

---

[1] See D. R. Shackleton Bailey, 'Some Recent Experiments in Propertian Criticism' in *Proceedings of the Cambridge Philological Society* (1952/3), 9ff.

[2] 'These sudden transitions, the allusiveness, the tortured syntax, are features of our modern poetry,' L. P. Wilkinson, in the oral discussion of P. Boyancé's lecture on Propertius, given under the auspices of the *Fondation Hardt* (vol. II, 1956, p. 219).

He has a strong sense, a clear perception of reality. His mythological erudition, heavy as it may appear at times, never suffocates this fresh vision of life that he wants to convey. Even where we have the impression that the *exempla* are accumulated for their own sake, they are never left hanging in the air. The beginning of the elegy mentioned above (1.3) provides a good illustration. Cynthia is compared first to Ariadne, then to Andromeda, and finally to a sleeping Bacchant. Each comparison is elaborated in a full distich. None of them really supersedes the two others. Ariadne symbolizes her loneliness; Andromeda her peaceful slumber after much worrying; and the Maenad suggests the outbreak of temperament of which she is capable.

Thus the mythological element in Propertius is never merely decorative. Aside from the concrete function it has in a given situation, from the light it throws on a given theme, it creates, as a whole, an almost religious atmosphere. Propertius *is* a religious poet; his idea of the poet is a sacerdotal one (4.6.1ff), and he wants his elegies (or at least most of them) to be read not only with absorption but with a kind of piety.

Roman religion comes to life in Propertius' 'Roman Elegies'. He celebrates Dionysus, the god of wine and poetry, in a hymn (3.17), and one of his last elegies, the dirge for Cornelia (4.11), is a deeply religious document. But these are works of Propertius' later years. As a young man he seems rather indifferent to organized religion. He is devoted to the 'religion of Love'. Mythology, in his earlier poems, is essentially an expression of his 'religion of Love'; for this reason it takes up such a large place in Book I.[1]

Tibullus and Propertius did not appeal to the same kind of reader. Since they were contemporaries, cultivating a relatively new kind of literature, their work naturally invited comparison. The critics must have asked: 'Who is our true elegist, our Roman Callimachus?' Propertius answered their question for them (4.1.64), but not all of them accepted his answer. By the time of Quintilian, the controversy had probably calmed down. Quintilian is less partial than Domitius Marsus; he offers the palm to Tibullus, but – *sunt qui Propertium malint.*

[1] On Propertius' 'religion of Love' and the role of mythology in his poetry, see V. Pöschl (above, n. 2), 216f.

It is still tempting to compare the two poets. At the danger of oversimplification one might say that they were as different as Terence and Plautus. Is it just coincidence that both Propertius and Plautus were natives of Umbria? They have much more in common than their origin; they share, above all, a feeling for life in its various dimensions, high and low, in its various colours. Their temperaments are exuberant, their minds experimental, their language full-blooded.

They came from different social classes. Plautus, it is said, worked for years as a stage-carpenter before he found recognition as a playwright. Propertius, whose family was of equestrian rank, met the right kind of people as soon as he came to Rome. But neither of them was attached to a literary circle when he wrote his first works or dependent on a patron to whose tastes he had to conform. In the case of Terence and Tibullus, it is clear that the influence of their patrons accounts, to a certain extent, for the character of their work. Both Terence and Tibullus adopt the *sermo purus*, which was a matter of course in the circles of Scipio and Messalla. Propertius used plebeian, or at least prosaic, words freely; while Tibullus carefully models his vocabulary on the *sermo urbanus*. Later, Propertius was invited by Maecenas to join his circle, but he already had a name and could not be expected to change his manner.

Both Tibullus and Propertius deal with the same range of emotions: love, despair, friendship, regret. The realm of both poets is the lyrical present. Their scenery, however, is different. Tibullus moves in an idealized landscape, one that never sinks to mere background, but harmonizes with the theme of his elegies, like a musical accompaniment. Propertius is the poet of the city, like Ovid, and there are very few bucolic themes in his poetry (2.19, 3.13, for example). On the other hand, there are few *pièces d'apparat* in Tibullus (1.7, 2.5).

The difference between the two poets could also be expressed by two contrasting rhetorical terms, *ethos* and *pathos*. There is more *ethos* in Tibullus, that is to say, he reveals indirectly more about his person and character than Propertius. He seems to think or dream aloud, inviting us to share his thoughts and reveries. Propertius has an urge to declaim; he likes to stand on a stage; he takes issues, points here and there, and his heated imagination spends itself on a thousand subjects. For this reason we seem to know Tibullus better than Delia, but Cynthia better than Propertius.

Tibullus' range of themes is somewhat limited. He feels at ease when he can abandon himself to a mood. Propertius, although no story-teller in the ordinary sense of the word, tries at least to find a beginning and an end. This applies to his affair with Cynthia as a whole (1.1 and 3.25), as well as the many stories, incidents and pointed situations that constitute its fabric. His technique is similar to that of the Greek novelists. There, a pair of lovers meet, usually during a festival, fall in love, promise each other eternal devotion, are separated by rivals, pirates and the like, fight various temptations, are reported dead to each other, decide to commit suicide, and are brought together by the benevolent gods at the last minute. Now Cynthia is fickle and faithless and there is no happy ending; but Propertius, like Heliodorus, Longus and their hypothetical Alexandrian models, leads the reader through a series of highly coloured dramatic incidents.

Ovid has learned this technique from Propertius. It is irrelevant to ask whether those incidents were based on personal experience. For all we know, they may have been largely adapted from Greek mythology, the poet taking the place of the protagonist (Theseus, Jason), his lady that of the heroine (Ariadne, Medea).

Both Ovid and Propertius share an interest in works of art (statues, painting) which is hardly noticeable in Tibullus. This may be purely accidental; it may, on the other hand, be intimately connected with their way of seeing things. Since all the poets of the Augustan Age were surrounded by works of art imported from Greece, it is perhaps significant that Ovid and Propertius noticed them more closely than others. Rome was a 'museum without walls' at that time; in private houses, temples, and on public places, there were illustrations to almost any Greek legend. The excavations of the last century have shown that even middle-class houses in Pompeii and Herculaneum were decorated with wall-paintings ultimately derived from Hellenistic originals.

It is difficult to decide in each given case whether a mythological reference in Propertius can be taken as a proof of the poet's familiarity with Greek art. We can never rule out the possibility that he knew the story from a book.

In 3.9.9ff Propertius lists the names of eight Greek artists. He seems to be familiar with the work of each. Lysippus, he says deserves praise for his realism (*animosa effingere signa*), Calamis for his consummate representations of horses; Apelles 'claims the primacy' (*summam sibi poscit*) in painting Aphrodite; Parrhasius is justly noted for his pictures in the *maniera piccola*; Mentor, Mys, Phidias and Praxiteles each have their qualities.

A very similar list occurs in one of Ovid's letters from the Black Sea (*Epistulae ex Ponto* 4.1.29ff). Ovid could not have the originals before his eyes when he wrote this, but he might have remembered Propertius' poem. His names are those of Propertius, except for Myron; but Myron's cow was almost proverbial.

Both poets include only the most famous names. Neither tells us anything new. Any educated Roman knew that much. But it is characteristic that both, in a completely different situation, rely on examples taken from the history of Greek art rather than from literature. Ovid, in an almost Byzantine compliment, uses them to prove that he is the 'property' of Sextus Pompeius just as much as these works are the property of their artists. Propertius is anxious to prove to Maecenas that he is not the man to write an epic poem; each artist, he implies, has his own domain.

Ovid visited Athens as a young man; Propertius plans a trip to Greece when he is already a well-known poet (2.21). He anticipates all the spiritual adventures that await him there: 'Paintings, at least, will catch my eyes, and works of art wrought in ivory or bronze,'

> *aut certe tabulae capient mea lumina pictae,*
> *sive ebore exactae, seu magis aere, manus.*
> (Propertius 3.21.29f)

This is a characteristic attitude. First of all, Propertius speaks as a tourist and connoisseur. Second, we note his desire for exactness; he wants to see both paintings and statues, and he distinguishes further what kinds of statues he expects to see. Third, there is a curious expression 'they will catch my eye'. It shows Propertius all ready to be excited visually, equipped with a fresh supply of enthusiasm that can hardly wait to embrace a beautiful object. This is not the attitude of Tibullus, who lets the things and persons of the external world drift toward him until they blend with the creatures of his imagination. A. G. Lee (*Gnomon* 1960, 518) has some very good remarks on this elegy: 'The lines (29f) are part of an artistic whole. *lumina* looks back to *spectando* (3) and *oculis* (10), just as *animum* looks back to *animo* (10). In addition *capient mea lumina* may possibly be meant to remind the reader of *Cynthia prima suis miserum me cepit ocellis*.'

It may seem strange that a poet like Propertius who is so intensely aware of the life which surrounds him, who apprehends its sights and sounds so readily, was at the same time haunted by visions of death. He likes to dwell with a kind of morbid pleasure on funerals and the underworld (1.19.6, 18; 2.13.42, 57f; 3.13.21f; 4.5.3f; 4.7.93f; 4.11.20, 37, 74). Unlike Tibullus he never lapses into self-pity when he thinks of his own death; on the contrary, he glories in the anticipation of an unusually dramatic and spectacular end. In a passionately bitter and vengeful poem (2.8), he accuses Cynthia of infidelity and then adds abruptly:

> Sic igitur prima moriere aetate, Properti?
>   sed morere; interitu gaudeat illa tuo!
> exagitat nostros Manis, sectetur et umbras,
>   insultetque rogis, calcet et ossa mea!
> quid? non Antigonae tumulo Boeotius Haemon
>   corruit ipse suo saucius ense latus,
> et sua cum miserae permiscuit ossa puellae,
>   qua sine Thebanam noluit ire domum?
> sed non effugies: mecum moriaris oportet;
>   hoc eodem ferro stillet uterque cruor.

'So, then, you will die in the prime of your life, Propertius? Yes, die you must – let her exalt in your death. Let her insult my Manes, pursue my shade, dance on my funeral pile and stamp on my bones. Did not Haemon of Boeotia die on the tomb of Antigone, pierced by his own sword, and mingle his bones with those of the unfortunate girl without whom he refused to go back to his house in Thebes? But you shall not escape – you must die with me; from this same blade must the blood of either drip.'

(2.8.17ff)

With a savage joy and a self-mortification that are highly characteristic of his personality, Propertius describes the final humiliation he expects to suffer from Cynthia. She will not only refuse to pay his Manes their share of mourning, but will gloat unashamedly over her lover's premature death. Even so, carried away by his anger and disgust, he cannot quite suppress a learned mythological allusion. While the vision of Antigone's fate is meant to provide comfort, it only pours oil into the flames of his wrath, goading him on to a sinister threat, stimulating his satisfaction at dramatizing himself in a tragic role.

It is not surprising that Propertius' wholehearted enjoyment of life is never far removed from the image of death.[1] In the middle of the most delighted description of sensual pleasure (2.15) he is suddenly reminded of the 'eternal night':

> *dum nos fata sinunt, oculos satiemus amore:*
> *nox tibi longa venit, nec reditura dies.*

'While the Fates grant it to us, let us fill our eyes with love-making; the long night comes for you, and daylight will never come back.'

> *tu modo, dum lucet, fructum ne desere vitae!*
> *omnia si dederis oscula, pauca dabis.*

'But you, do not fail to do justice to the enjoyment of life as long as the light shines. You may have given me all your kisses; they will be all too few.'

(2.15.23f, 49f)

These lines reflect not so much the fear that all this present bliss might end too soon, as the desire to squeeze the last drop of enjoyment out of it by contrasting it to physical extinction.[2]

The ideas of love and death are closely connected in Propertius. Only the lover knows how and when he will die:

> *solus amans novit, quando periturus et a qua*
> *morte . . .*

(2.27.11f)

[1] Agnes Kirsopp Michels has given a good treatment of the death theme in Lucretius and Propertius, in *Trans. and Proc. of the Am. Philol. Ass.* (1955), 171ff.

[2] The same thought appears elsewhere in Latin erotic poetry, Catullus 5.4-6; Tibullus 1.1.69f; Ovid, *Amores* 2.9.42.

even though his death may come unexpectedly to his friends:

> *ambulat – et subito mirantur funus amici.*

'He walks along – and suddenly his friends are surprised to see that he is dead!'

(2.4.13)

All ancient poetry is, in an essential sense, poetry of celebration. A hero's deeds, a woman's beauty, the power of friendship or love, would be meaningless without the praise which the poet alone can bestow upon them. Just as love was the guiding force during his lifetime, it will transcend the tomb after Propertius' death:

> *non adeo leviter nostris puer haesit ocellis*
> *ut meus oblito pulvis amore vacet.*

'Not so lightly has Love clung to my eyes that my dust could forget love and lie loveless.'[1]

(1.19.5f)

This thought takes an extraordinary form in a later poem. The lover's shade is crouching in the reeds at the banks of the river Styx, waiting to be shipped over, when he suddenly hears his mistress' voice from the world of the living. And so strong is her power over him that he will return 'over the road that the eternal ordinance has closed',

> *iam licet et Stygia sedeat sub harundine remex,*
> *cernat et infernae tristia vela ratis:*
> *si modo clamantis revocaverit aura* puellae,*
> *concessum nulla lege redibit iter.*

(2.27.13ff)

* (MSS.: *revocarint ora* Markland)

Is this not the situation of Orpheus and Eurydice in reverse? In the legend Orpheus' urgent appeals won back Eurydice in spite of the 'eternal laws'. In Propertius' vision, the *domina* takes on

[1] *Noster puer* is the reading accepted by most editors on good authority; *nostris* is an early correction in one MS.; it can be defended on the following grounds: (*a*) *puer* needs no qualification, as it is followed by *amore* in the next line; (*b*) the possessive pronoun with *ocellis* (although pleonastic) occurs also in 1.1.1.

the role of Orpheus, while the man who is in love with her has suffered Eurydice's fate.

This odd inversion of the relationship between man and woman is found elsewhere in Propertius. In the *Iliad* Andromache reminds Hector, who is leaving for the battle, that he is 'father to me, and my honoured mother, my brother, too; and it is you who are my young husband' (6.429). Propertius says to Cynthia

> *tu mihi sola domus, tu, Cynthia, sola parentes,*

'you, Cynthia, alone, are my family, you alone my parents.'
(1.11.23)

It is an extraordinary innovation in a traditional formula, and a radical break with the Alexandrian poetic tradition.[1] No Alexandrian poet could have attributed so much importance to a woman. In Rome this was possible; the role of the woman in Rome society was much more respected. Thus the mistress becomes the *domina*, the lover her 'slave' (a metaphor which is as rare in Greek erotic poetry as it is frequent in Latin elegiac verse). The earliest evidence for this 'inversion' is found in Catullus; Propertius goes one step further by extending the power of the *domina* beyond the grave:

> *illic quidquid ero, semper tua dicar imago:*
> *traicit et fati litora magnus amor.*

'There (in the underworld), whatever I shall be, my shade will always be known as your property; great love transcends even the shores of death.'
(1.19.11f)

> *huius ero vivus, mortuus huius ero.*

'I shall be her property alive – dead I shall be hers.'
(2.15.36)

Propertius is deeply concerned with life after death. It is interesting to see how different concepts exist, for a while at least, side by side in his mind. There is the traditional image of Hades, with Cerberus guarding the entrance (4.11.25f), with

---

[1] F. Klingner, in the discussion mentioned above, 212.

the Styx across which the dead are ferried or have to row
(2.27.13f; 4.7.55ff; 11.7; 15f); there are the judges of the
underworld, Aeacus presiding (4.11.19f); there are the great
sinners, Sisyphus, Ixion, Tantalus who have to expiate for ever
the crimes they committed on earth (3.5.39ff; 4.11.23ff).
But Propertius does not really know whether to believe all this.
In his old age, 'when the burdening years have set a stay to love,'
he expects to think about the answers that the philosophers have
given, and then he will make up his mind as to whether he had
not better accept Epicurus' thesis that all these tales are fictitious
and that 'fear cannot exist beyond the funeral pyre' (3.5.39ff).

But did he ever make up his mind? Did he become an Epicurean,
after all? I think there is some evidence in 3.18, the elegy on the
death of Marcellus, that the poet stayed attached to the traditional
ideas, though with an important modification that shows philosophical influence.

After death, three separate entities remain of the individual:
corpus (σῶμα), umbra (εἴδωλον) and anima (ψυχή). The
body falls to dust and ashes, the shadow departs for the underworld and carries on a pseudo-existence, while the soul flies up
to the celestial spheres. This is the concept of πολυψυχία.[1] It
can be traced back to archaic Greece, and its function is clearly
to reconcile the traditional image of Hades with the hopes of
those who were initiated into the Orphic or Eleusinian Mysteries
and were looking forward to a blessed life. Originally it was
believed that only the heroes and demi-gods could enjoy immortality. But the circle of those who were privileged in this way must
have grown, and in Hellenistic times it seems to have included
not only those who were initiated into the various mystery
religions, but also great statesmen, great poets, artists and
philosophers. Cicero's *Somnium Scipionis*, based on the work of
a late Hellenistic philosopher, reflects this view. Propertius
addresses himself to the deified *Manes* of Callimachus and
Philetas (3.1.1ff), and it is clear that a noble young Roman like
Augustus' nephew Marcellus who has shown great promise is
also a hero and that his soul will dwell in the heavenly regions
(3.18.3ff):

[1] Cf. E. Rohde, *Psyche* 1460; *Kleine Schriften* II 255ff; F. Cumont, *Lux Perpetua*
1949, 408.

at tibi, nauta, pias hominum qui traicis umbras,
  hoc animae portent corpus inane suae:
qua Siculae victor telluris Claudius et qua
  Caesar, ab humano cessit in astra via.

In spite of his noble birth, position, and youth, Marcellus had to die; but only his shade will enter Hades; his soul, his true self, like that of his illustrious ancestor Marcus Claudius Marcellus, the conqueror of Syracuse, has left the human sphere and joined the stars.

8

Sacra Facit Vates

Of the elegiac poets, only Propertius has made a serious and sustained effort to discuss the nature and principles of his art. Like Horace, he seems continually to underline the dignity and difficulty of his task. He is very much aware of his role as an innovator; it was only natural that he should be busy charting the new domain of letters that he claimed for himself. Unlike Horace, Propertius has never written an essay on literary criticism; his *ars poetica* must be reconstructed from a few programmatic poems and many scattered remarks.

Tibullus was not particularly keen to talk about literature; he felt, perhaps, that when a poet loses his innocence, his charm goes with it. And when Ovid reflects on poetry and the mission of the poet in society, he almost invariably uses the ready-made arguments and images that he found in Propertius.

What is elegiac poetry? Why do I have to write elegies? Who are my readers, and how do they respond to my verse? These are some of the questions that seem to haunt Propertius' mind. As a young man, he had known success, but he was never quite satisfied with the spontaneous recognition he found so early in his life. As the legitimate successor of Callimachus and Philetas, he is *poeta doctus* – scholar and critic as well as poet – and thus unwilling to take his own talent for granted, without subjecting it to close scrutiny. Once Maecenas takes a personal interest in him and starts encouraging him to write an epic poem, he feels compelled to stress the limitations of his talent.

Throughout his life, Propertius has been fascinated by the problem of poetic creation. To him, this subject is so mysterious and important that he has to resort to imagery and symbolism whenever he tries to come to terms with it. Unlike Horace in the *Ars Poetica* he does not talk about the technical aspects of writing poetry, but about the importance of being a poet.

The critic who seeks to interpret Propertius' imagery is placed at a serious disadvantage. None of his images has any given, permanent 'meaning'. It is dangerous to read between the lines. Propertius' peculiar art lies in the communication of feeling – a poetic gift, at bottom, which can easily be obscured by too much scholarship.

This in itself is no easy task. We have at our disposal two new editions, one of which is reliable[1]; the other, at least adequate,[2] if used with caution; and an admirable book of interpretations that includes practically all the controversial passages in Propertius and throws light on many more.[3] There is still no completely satisfactory modern translation. I have attempted, therefore, to render into English all the significant passages that I had to quote. Propertius is no smooth and elegant poet; for this reason, I have sacrificed every pretence at elegance and smoothness in favour of a close, literal translation.

What does it mean to be a poet? It means to participate in knowledge that is denied to the *profanum vulgus*. This knowledge is revealed to the poet by Apollo and the Muses.[4] He is their *sacerdos*, priest and prophet in one. Every new poem is based on a new revelation and marks a new beginning. I am not implying that Propertius actually *believed* that he wrote by divine inspiration. When he claims to have encountered Apollo and the Muses on Mount Helicon, he does not expect to be taken literally. But he *does* believe in the mission of the poet and in his right to follow his own chosen path. The poet may feel indebted to certain literary models (Callimachus and Philetas); but his inspiration is a mysterious gift and justifies his claim to walk on an untrodden path:

[1] E. A. Barber (Oxford, Clarendon Press 1953).

[2] M. Schuster – F. Dornseiff (Leipzig, Teubner 1954).

[3] D. R. Shackleton Bailey, *Propertiana* (Cambridge Univ. Pr. 1954).

[4] On the religious meaning of poetic inspiration in Antiquity see E. R. Dodds, *The Greeks and the Irrational* (California Univ. Pr. 1951), 80f; G. Luck, *Gnomon* (1953), 465. On the imagery of Prop. 3.1-3 cf. G. Luck, *Class. Quart.* 1957, 175ff.

primus ego ingredior puro de fonte sacerdos
Itala per Graios orgia ferre choros.[1]

'I am the first, the priest from a pure source, to take my way and carry Italian mystic symbols[2] among Greek dances.'

(3.1.3f)

It is Propertius' desire to lift the poet out of his place in ordinary life and to ascribe to him the function of a priest and prophet. Every work of literature, according to his view, represents a new revelation. The worship of the Muses was at first a privilege of the Greeks; Propertius writes in Latin, but follows the Greek literary tradition.

This does not mean that he is a mere translator; on the contrary, like Callimachus, he has been prepared for his task on Mount Helicon:

sed, quod pace legas, opus hoc de monte sororum
detulit intacta pagina nostra via.

'But this work which you may read in times of peace, my page[3] has brought down from the mount of the Muses by an untrodden[4] path.'

(3.1.17f)

Callimachus, too, the master whom he invokes so often, had his writing-tablet ready, when Apollo spoke to him.[5] As a record of an authentic revelation, that 'page' is more than just a page of verse; it represents the whole personality of the inspired poet.

[1] The true poet is an innovator, εὑρετής; this claim occurs frequently in Hellenistic literature (G. Luck, *Museum Helveticum*, 1954, 185), and such passages as Callimachus, *Aitia* I, fr. 1.25ff (Pf.); *Hy.* 2.110ff; *Ep.* 28.1f have found an echo in Roman poetry. See the commentary of Butler and Barber.

[2] The same 'mystic symbols' (*Musarum sacra*, Vergil, *Georgica* 2.475ff) decorate the grotto of the Muses in 3.3.29 (if one substitutes Heinsius' plausible correction for MS. *ergo*; Wilamowitz and others defend the conjecture *organa* and think of musical instruments).

[3] On the meaning of this metaphor see the commentators on 4.6.3 and p. 138, n. 2 below.

[4] Callimachus, *Aitia* I, fr. 1.25ff (Pf.); *Ep.* 7.1.

[5] Callimachus, *Aitia* I, fr. 1.21f.

Poetry is not a broad and comfortable highway, but a narrow path:

> non datur ad Musas currere lata via.[1]
>
> (3.1.14)

Not everyone can be a Callimachus or a Propertius. The ascent to Helicon is steep, but the reward rich. In a dream, Phoebus himself has shown Propertius a new path leading to the grotto of the Muses, where he could see their mystic symbols hanging from the wall (3.3.25ff).[2]

When Propertius talks about his inspiration, he feels that his whole being is enlarged, and the joy of creating poetry is to him like a religious experience. Plain words cannot describe this feeling; he needs ever new images to capture his sense of a sacred mission. At the beginning of 2.10, he announces an epic poem in honour of Rome's victories. He encourages himself to carry out this new endeavour:

> sed tempus lustrare aliis Helicona choreis
> et campum Haemonio iam dare tempus equo.

'But it is time to range with other dances over Helicon, and time now to launch the Thessalian[3] horse over the plain.'

> (2.10.1ff)

The dance is one of the characteristic images for poetic creation in Propertius. The appeal of a ballet performance consists in the perfect co-ordination of music, movement and gesture. The choreography may be complex and difficult, but the final impression must be one of natural elegance. Propertius has imposed the standards of Alexandrian poetry, the discipline of the elegiac metre on Roman verse. The success of his poetry represents a triumph over these self-imposed standards:

[1] Cf. 3.9.8, palma nec ex aequo ducitur una iugo, 'from heights unequal men bring down different palms'; 4.10.3f, magnum iter ascendo, sed dat mihi gloria (= studium laudis) vires: non iuvat e facili lecta corona iugo.

[2] See below, p. 141.

[3] According to Wilamowitz, Hellenist. Dicht. II, 93, n. 2, this epithet shows regrettable 'lack of taste'; it is meaningless, he thinks, and suggested by learned, not to say, pedantic associations. This criticism is exaggerated. The poet simply prefers the concrete to the abstract.

> *me iuvet[1] in prima coluisse Helicona iuventa*
> *Musarumque choris implicuisse manus.*

'Let it be my delight to have worshipped Helicon in my earliest youth, and to have joined hands in the Muses' dance.'

(3.5.19f)

In an earlier poem, he expands this simple image to a word-conscious, metaphor-charged narrative. He invites Cynthia to join him on a trip to Helicon. There the Muses are dancing on the rocks, singing mythical love-songs, for 'they are not ignorant of what it means to be in love'. They will place Cynthia in the foremost row of their ballet, with Bacchus as *Musagetes*, holding his thyrsus staff, standing in the middle, and Propertius himself ready to accept a garland of holy ivy clusters:

> *Hic ubi te[2] prima statuent in parte choreae*
> *et medius docta cuspide Bacchus erit,*
> *tum capiti sacros patiar pendere corymbos. . . .*

(2.30.37ff)

The idealized landscape that the poet sees returns once more, in a dream, in 3.3. Now, Bacchus, who plays such a prominent role as god of poetry,[3] is absent – or rather, he is represented by the terra-cotta busts of Pan and Silenus. His 'wand of song', the symbol of poetic inspiration, takes the place of the laurel-staff which Hesiod once received as a gift from the Muses. One symbol is not enough for Propertius; he adds the ivy garland, the 'soft wreath', for his head is not made for the thorny garland of the epic poet.[4] It is significant that Propertius introduces Cynthia into the ballet of the Muses – an exquisite compliment to the woman who has given him his *ingenium*.[5] She is now the tenth Muse and enjoys a privilege usually reserved to Sappho.[6]

He is equally fond of another image for the creative process.

---

[1] Bürger's correction of *iuvat* (MSS.), accepted now by Schuster-Dornseiff (cf. v. 21).   [2] *te* (codd. dett.) accepted by the more recent editors.

[3] Cf. 3.2.9f; 4.1.62, 6.75f; E. Maass, *Hermes* (1896), 376ff, 386.

[4] Cf. 3.1.19f; 4.1.61, *Ennius hirsuta cingat sua dicta corona.*

[5] Cf. 2.1.4, 30.40, and above, p. 112.

[6] Antipater Sidon., *Anth. Pal.* 7.14; Antipater Thess., *Anth. Pal.* 9.26 (Luck, *Museum Helveticum*, 1954, 170; 171, n. 8); and on Erinna who 'joins in the dance of the Muses', anon., *Anth. Pal.* 7.12.6 (Luck 171, n. 8; 185, n. 86).

The race implies a movement; it is swift and powerful, as the dance was graceful and ordered. In the beginning of 2.10, the image changed abruptly from the ballet (v. 1) to the fields of song, over which the poet guides his chariot (v. 2). Pindar once spoke of the 'four-horsed chariot of the Muses'.[1] In 3.1 Propertius expands this concept. He has a vision of his chariot, *currus*, the tender Love-gods riding in it, and the band of his literary rivals[2] following behind, each on his own chariot, it seems, each racing at full speed toward the temple of the Muses – but in vain:

> *quid frustra missis[3] in me certatis habenis?*

'Why do you in vain, with loosened reins, compete with me?'

(3.1.13)

Fame has lent wings to Propertius; he soars high above the earth,

> *quo me Fama levat terra sublimis.*[4]

(3.1.9)

But without a transition, the image changes again; the car that was already sailing through the air on the wings of Fame is really on the ground and moves in a triumphal procession.[5] On it stands the Muse, child of the poet's genius, driven by garlanded horses:

> *et a me*
> *nata coronatis Musa triumphat equis.*

'and the Muse who is born of me[6] triumphs with garlanded horses.'

(3.1.9f)

A poem on the nature of inspiration needs a host of images. Each image holds within it the seed of its own destruction. Propertius' method consists in a constant building up and breaking down of images. The *imitatorum servum pecus* again has its place in

---

[1] Pindar, *Py.* 10.65; cf. *Ol.* 9.81.

[2] *scriptorum turba*; cf. v. 21, *invida turba*; 4.1.136, *cetera turba*.

[3] On *missis=emissis* (the simplex for the compositum) see E. Löfstedt, *Vermischte Studien* (1936), 121, n. 1.

[4] Cf. Theognis 237f; Pindar, *Isthm.* 1.64, and the commentators.

[5] A similar change of imagery occurs in a related passage, Vergil, *Georgica* 3.9ff.

[6] The same metaphor (birth of a song) in Callimachus, *Aitia* I, fr. 1.19f (Pf.).

this new scene. They are the soldiers of the victorious general (or, perhaps, his prisoners) who walk behind the chariot.[1]

In another poem, Propertius has taken the place of his Muse on the chariot. He is careful to drive over 'delicate lawns':

> *mollia sunt parvis prata terenda rotis.*

'little wheels must roll over soft meadows.'

(3.3.18)

The vehicle of his *ingenium*[2] is not equipped for the rough terrain of epic poetry; it will break down as soon as he ventures outside of the familiar pastures of elegiac verse. Even the reins of this vehicle are soft, as he once reminds Maecenas:

> *mollia[3] tu coeptae fautor cape lora iuventae*
> *dexteraque immissis da mihi signa rotis.*

'Patron of my first youth, take the pliant reins and give me the favouring signs when my wheels break into full speed.'

(3.9.57f)

Within the same distich, the image has changed again. In the hexameter, Maecenas himself is the driver. As Propertius' patron, he will win the race for him. In the pentameter, however, Maecenas appears to be a distinguished spectator, encouraging Propertius, his favourite driver, at the beginning of the race.

Later in life, when he is ready to embark upon a new poetic project, Propertius uses this image once more. In the first elegy of the last book, announcing a series of antiquarian elegies, he adds:

> *sacra diesque canam et cognomina prisca locorum:*
> *has meus ad metas sudet oportet equus.*

---

[1] Ovid has adapted the whole passage in *Amores* 1.2.23-38; but he follows at the same time a Greek model (E. Rohde, *Der griech. Roman*, 115, n. 1). In his elegy, it is not the poet nor the Muse, but Cupid who acts as *triumphator* (instead of being a harmless playmate or companion, as in Propertius), while the poet himself, dramatically enough, follows behind the chariot, as a prisoner in chains. Other prisoners, young men and women, take the place of Propertius' imitators. Ovid's description is more colourful – an ἔκφρασις in the Alexandrian manner – and a little ironical.

[2] Later (v. 21) identified with the *pagina*, his life as it is reflected in his work, cf. 3.1.18, 4.6.3.

[3] Broekhuyzen's correction of MS. *mollis*, convincingly defended by Shackleton Bailey.

'I shall make a song of rites and their days and of ancient names of places; this must be the goal toward which my sweating horse shall run.'[1]

$$(4.1.69f)$$

These lines inaugurate a new phase of his career. For the first time, the context suggests an effort (the horse is sweating). Love-poetry came to him naturally; it was like riding in a winged car or being lifted up by white swans:

> contentus niveis semper vectabere[2] cycnis,
> nec te fortis equi ducet ad arma sonus.

'You should always ride contentedly upon snow-white swans, and the din of a gallant horse should not carry you into battle.'

$$(3.3.39f)$$

Venus lent her own birds to the love-poet to facilitate his task. Now he needs the horse.

Propertius likes to speak about the dignity of his mission. He is proud of what he has achieved, but a little embarrassed by the limitations of his talent. He may have been secretly envious of other members of Maecenas' circle, whose versatility impressed him. Both Vergil and Horace were at home in various provinces of literature. Ovid, outside the circle, but a friend of his, showed both promise and inclination for epic and tragedy, after having made his début as a writer of love-elegies. Throughout Propertius' work, we find this quarrel with himself, this constant urge to explain, to justify his own limited experience, his inability to leave the native domain of elegiac verse. He is perpetually searching for new symbols that might convey to the reader a sense of his own dilemma:

> nondum etiam Ascraeos norunt mea carmina fontes,
> sed modo Permessi flumine lavit Amor.

'My songs have not yet come to know the sources of Ascra; Love has but dipped them in Permessus' stream.'[3]

$$(2.10.25f)$$

[1] Cf. Ovid, Amores 3.15.18, pulsanda est magnis area maior equis, also announcing a new and more elevated kind of poetry.

[2] The future has the function of an imperative.

[3] On the interpretation of this difficult couplet see above, E. Maass, Hermes (1896), 391, 425; Rothstein in his comment., I[2], 476ff; Wilamowitz, Hellenist.

To understand this distich, we have to distinguish two ideas: one, that drinking from a sacred source is intended as a symbol for poetic inspiration; and second, that the epic and didactic poets do not receive their inspiration at the same place as the elegists. The stream of Permessus runs through the valley at the foot of Helicon, while the *fontes* of Hesiod, whatever they are, must be higher up, since they are clearly contrasted with the *flumen*. The difference in altitude suggests a difference in style; the *genus sublime*, 'the grand manner', is contrasted with the *genus tenue*, the 'humble manner'. It is useless to bring into this discussion the topography of Helicon, of which Propertius and other poets had only a vague conception. When he names realities, he usually acknowledges an obligation to make his symbols rich, and more often than not, he is seduced by felicitous sound values.

A similar distinction occurs in a later poem, 3.3. Propertius has grown more ambitious. A dream has carried him on to Mount Helicon; he finds himself near the Hippocrene. He remembers that once, before embarking on the *Annales*, Ennius enjoyed hearty draughts from this source. Propertius has made up his mind to follow Ennius' example; he bends down to drink from 'those mighty fountains'; but the water gushes forth too violently:

> *parvaque tam magnis admoram fontibus ora,*
> *unde pater sitiens Ennius ante bibit.*

'and I had set my puny mouth to those mighty fountains, whence Father Ennius before quenched his thirst.'

(3.3.5f)

At this moment Apollo interrupts him with an urgent warning:

> *quid tibi cum tali, demens, est flumine? quis te*
> *carminis heroi tangere iussit opus?*

'Madman, what business do you have with such a stream? Who asked you to attempt the task of the heroic poem?'

(3.3.15f)

The answer, barely implied by the poet, is: It was Maecenas. The command of a mortal stands against that of a god. In the form of

---

Dicht. II, 94ff; Kirsten, RE 19.869; E. Reitzenstein, *Festschrift R. Reitzenstein* (1931), *passim*; Pfeiffer's note on Call. Schol. ad fr. 2 (p. 11, cf. Add. vol. II) and on fr. 696.

a prophecy, Apollo further discourages Propertius from trying his hand at epic poetry (3.3.15-24).[1] In a parallel speech of almost equal length (3.3.39-50), the Muse, Calliope, elaborates on the same theme and, drawing water from a spring, moistens the poet's lips with the 'water of Philetas':

> talia Calliope, lymphisque a fonte petitis
> ora Philetaea nostra rigavit aqua.

(3.3.51f)

The 'water of Philetas' (and Callimachus) is a new symbol. Hippocrene had inspired Ennius, but this other source is reserved to the elegiac poet. It has no name in Propertius, but its function is underlined by the idyllic surroundings, and the pretty doves dipping their purple beaks 'into the Gorgon pool' (3.3.31f). This pool, as the name suggests, must be connected with the Hippocrene, but it is a pool, not a source, possibly a natural cavity in the ground, where the water that gushed forth so powerfully from Hippocrene now forms a quiet little lake, safe even for doves to drink from. It is the same water that the epic poet tastes higher up, as it springs from the ground, before it has become tame and civilized, before it becomes the 'water of Philetas'. The pool from which the 'birds of my lady, Venus, my favourite company,' (3.3.31) are drinking, derives its water from Hippocrene, just as the elegy, metrically speaking, is 'derived' from the epic. There is only one source from which all inspiration flows, but there is an easier and more difficult access to it.[2]

Propertius was born in a small town. His family is undistinguished. He could never be successful in the conventional sense

[1] Cf. Apollo's advice to Callimachus, *Aitia* I, fr. 1.23ff (Pf.) (and the parallels in Augustan poetry, listed by Pfeiffer ad loc.).

[2] See above, p. 139f, on the distinction between *fons* and *flumen* in 2.10.25f. Most critics have failed to see that in this poem an analogous distinction is made between *fontes* (v. 5) and *lacus* (v. 32); recently, Schuster-Dornseiff have explained *Gorgoneus lacus* as Hippocrene itself – a serious error, especially after E. Reitzenstein's lucid discussion.

Two simple facts have been obscured by the number of over-subtle interpretations which have accumulated around this passage: (1) the difference in altitude (*fons*, higher – *flumen* and *lacus*, lower) corresponds to a difference of elevation in style; (2) the water of the source is powerful, swift, fresh, but farther down it moves slowly, is tame and somewhat tepid.

of the word, as a soldier or politician. But his *ingenium* brought
him recognition and a comfortable life:

> *aspice me, cui parva domi fortuna relicta est*
> *nullus et antiquo Marte triumphus avi,*
> *ut regnem mixtas inter conviva puellas*
> *hoc ego, quo tibi nunc elevor, ingenio!*
> *me iuvet hesternis positum languere corollis,*
> *quem tetigit iactu certus ad ossa deus.*

$$(2.34.55\text{ff})$$

Even at Rome, he had found a social structure capable of being
an aid to works of imagination: 'Look at me, to whom only a
small fortune has been left at home,[1] and no triumph of an
ancestor in some ancient war – how I rule as a king at the table
among a party of girls,[2] thanks to this genius of mine which you
do not now take seriously. Let it be my delight to lie languidly
under the wreaths of last night,[3] pierced to the bone by the shot
of the god who does not miss his mark.' The small range of his
themes may be held against him by his contemporaries, poets and
critics alike. Horace's *sermones* dealt with moral questions in a
shrewd and amusing fashion; Vergil's *Aeneid* revived Rome's past
in grandiose colours; Propertius writes well only when he writes
about himself.[4]

Knowing these limitations of his talent, Propertius often seems
to worry about the response of his readers. The *Monobiblos* had
established his success. But he claims that he writes for eternity,
not for ephemeral recognition. Still, he needs the certainty that
he has something significant to say to his contemporaries. Where
is my public, he seems to ask; who reads me and why?

Above all, he is writing for Cynthia. She is his favourite audience:

> *me iuvat in gremio doctae legisse puellae,*
> *auribus et puris scripta probasse mea.*

[1] Cf. 3.5.3-6.   [2] Cf. 3.2.9f.   [3] Cf. 2.15.41f, 3.5.21f.
[4] Wine and good companionship are other ingredients of the successful literary
work of art, cf. 4.6.75f, *ingenium positis* (NFL, Barber, Schuster-Dornseiff: *potis* DV,
Phillimore) *irritet Musa poetis: Bacche, soles Phoebo fertilis esse tuo*; see p. 136 above;
Lygdamus 4.43f; Ovid, *Amores* 1.3.7ff. Did Propertius know that Callimachus and
his followers were 'water-drinkers' (Antipater Thess., *Anth. Pal.* 11.20; 31) and
that the master himself had spoken disdainfully of Archilochus as μεθυπλήξ, 'wine-
stricken' (fr. 544, Pf.)?

'It is my pleasure to read (my verse) in the lap of a cultured girl, and have her pure ears approve what I have written.'

(2.13.11f)

We saw above that he had other female admirers. On their book-shelves, his elegies stood next to those of Callimachus and Philetas:

> inter Callimachi sat erit placuisse libellos,
>   et cecinisse modis, Coe poeta, tuis.
> haec urant pueros, haec urant scripta puellas,
>   meque deum clament et mihi sacra ferant!

'Enough for me to have found acceptance among the books of Callimachus, and to have sung in your manner, poet of Cos. Let these writings inflame the boys, let them inflame the girls,[1] and let them acclaim me as a god and offer worship to me.'

(3.9.43ff)

The elegiac poet has abstracted novel and significant patterns from a range of experience accessible to all of his readers. The more they learn about his love, the more meaning they find in their own. Poetry imitates life; life imitates poetry.

Once or twice Propertius has in mind a solitary reader. He imagines a girl who is waiting for her lover, reading a few pages of Propertius to while away the hours; then, hearing a noise, she drops the book and leaps up:

> ut tuus in scamno[2] iactetur saepe libellus,
>   quem legat exspectans sola puella virum.

---

[1] Recently Shackleton Bailey, ad loc., has made a good case for a new interpretation of v. 45, urant. He takes the fire to be not love but imitation. Propertius writes for youthful readers, 1.7.23, and expects them to follow his example. This seems plausible. If one understands urant in this sense, the transition to v. 46 appears less forced. They worship Propertius because he is a great poet. It seems a little odd, however, to mention the puellae together with the pueri as potential poets, although Cynthia wrote poetry herself.

[2] On the abl. where we expect the acc. see Kühner-Stegmann I, 592, and the additional comments of Shackleton Bailey, 296.

'so that your book is frequently thrown on the footstool –
your book, which a girl, while she waits for her lover, alone,
is reading.'[1]

(3.3.19f)

The romantic part of Propertius' work is an adolescent's day-
dream – gay and sad, frivolous and tragic. Its charm and freshness
endear him to a youthful reader, particularly when the poet has
found words that seem to come from his own heart. The appeal
of this love-poetry lies in its universality.[2] Although his love for
Cynthia is in the foreground, Propertius is not trying to picture –
autobiographically, as it were – one person's passion, but the
typical lover's love. Reality is transformed to suit a more general
theme.

That he found unfriendly critics, could only be expected. Once
he speaks with contempt of the *populi confusa fabula* (2.13.13f),
the 'confusion of common talk', irrelevant as long as the *docta
puella* approves of his verse. On the whole, he counts with a large
audience and a throng of imitators. But fame can have its unpleasant aspects. He complains that he is too much talked about at
Rome. His breathless sincerity seems to embarrass certain readers:

> '*Tu loqueris, cum sis iam noto fabula libro*
>   *et tua sit toto Cynthia lecta foro?*'
> *cui non his verbis aspergat tempora sudor?*
>   *aut pudor ingenuis aut retinendus amor.*
> *quod si iam facilis spiraret Cynthia nobis,*
>   *non ego nequitiae dicerer esse caput,*
> *nec sic per totam infamis traducerer urbem,*
>   *urerer et quamvis non bene, verba darem.*

'"Who are you to talk, when you are already the talk of the
town, after your book has become known and your 'Cynthia'
read all over the Forum?"'[3] Whose temples would not be
sprinkled with sweat at these words? Gentlemen must keep

[1] Strato, *Anth. Pal.* 12.208.5ff, addressing his book which is read by a *puer
delicatus*, 'Often will you slide into his bosom, or, tossed down on his chair . . . and
you will talk much before him, all alone with him . . .'; Ovid, *Amores* 2.1.5.

[2] Cf. 1.7.13, *me legat assidue post haec neglectus amator.*

[3] He begins, as often, with the speech of an imaginary interlocutor. On the 'talk
of the town' cf. Ovid, *Amores* 3.1.21f. Text and interpretation of this difficult
passage after Shackleton Bailey, 110ff.

either self-respect or love. Yet, if you would breathe gently at me,[1] Cynthia, I would not be called the fountain-head of worthlessness, nor would I be exposed, as I am, to laughter all over the city. However badly I might be burned, I would cheat the public.'

$$(2.24.1\text{ff})$$

The conventional Roman mind demanded that poetry be moral or useful and not only discredited the artist's function, but was inclined to outlaw the artist. In the eyes of some of his readers, Propertius has become a mere performer, an exhibitionist. He is now labelled as the romantic who glories in the sickness of love as a long sweet disease. Writing about his love for Cynthia, he revealed too much of himself and lost part of his personal *dignitas*. The secrets of the boudoir have become a topic of conversation on the Forum; and Propertius himself pretends to regret this *succès de scandale*.

Propertius is too much a Roman at heart to treat the poet's function in society lightly. He feels that the *vates* should be concerned with moral as well as aesthetic issues. Horace distinguished a twofold aim of any literary work of art: *aut prodesse volunt aut delectare poetae*, adding that a blend of the *utile* and *dulce* represented the highest achievement. Horace's statement reflects the climate of literary opinion in the circle of Maecenas. Regardless of his personal relations with Horace, these were the standards that Propertius had to keep in mind.

Again, he is painfully aware of his real or imaginary shortcomings. Was it enough that he practised art for art's sake, that he found self-fulfilment in his poetry?

> *illorum antiquis onerantur legibus aures :*
> *hic locus est in quo, tibia docta, sones . . .*

'the ears of those men (the *senes duri* of v. 13) are burdened by ancient laws; there is a place here, where you, accomplished flute, may sound . . .'

$$(2.30.15\text{f})$$

In spite of this proud assertion, he often betrays a certain uneasiness when he speaks about the proper role of the poet. Does

[1] Cf. Tibullus 2.1.80; Theocritus 12.10.

he really do justice to his talent? Is it enough just to write love-poems?

He knows that his poetry is read for its ingratiating quality. It is *blandum* and *molle*, 'gentle' and 'soft'. It represents a triumph of literary craftsmanship. It appeals to adolescents in love because they hear the voice of their own experience. But is it *utile*, 'useful', in the concrete Roman sense of the word?

> *possum ego diversos iterum coniungere amantis*
> *et dominae tardas possum aperire fores;*
> *et possum alterius curas sanare recentis,*
> *nec levis in verbis est medicina meis.*

'I have power to join parted lovers again, and power to open up the reluctant doors of the mistress, and power to heal another man's fresh sorrows[1]' nor is there a small remedy in my words.'

(1.10.15ff)

His own experience has prepared him to give advice to the love-lorn; but his poetry is more than advice; it is magic, verbal incantation. Propertius speaks of his powers in terms which occur more frequently in descriptions of witchcraft. The therapeutic value of love-poetry is greater than that of philosophical books:

> *quid tua Socraticis tibi nunc sapientia libris*
> *proderit aut rerum dicere posse vias?*

'What good will the wisdom of Socratic volumes do to you now, or your ability to discuss the ways of nature?'

(2.34.27f)

To study Greek philosophy, to apply the Platonic θεραπεία ψυχῆς, is a waste of time, if you are in love. Propertius affirms here and elsewhere that he has not entered an atmosphere too rarefied, except for the few. He declines the obvious charge that he is only speaking of himself and to himself and insists that he is speaking to his fellow-man. 'In love, the line of Mimnermus is worth more than Homer,' he asserts in an early poem (1.9.11).[2]

Shortly afterwards, he seems to have lost this confidence.

---

[1] Cf. 1.7.13.   [2] See above, p. 32f.

'Medicine cures all human pains, love alone has no specialist for its disease,'

> *omnis humanos sanat medicina dolores,*
> *solus amor morbi non habet artificem.*[1]

$$(2.2.57f)$$

As a 'teacher of love'[2] for others he may be successful; as a man in love he is helpless. It is through contradictions such as these that Propertius interests us and reveals his sincerity.

During the Augustan Age, certain conventions were shared by almost all the poets. Certain themes, certain rhetorical figures, certain images went along with elegy, certain others with epic poetry. Propertius could expect his readers to understand immediately how any one elegy he wrote was to be 'taken'. On the whole, his poetry claims to be practical. Ingratiating and persuasive, it addresses itself to the Roman *jeunesse dorée*. It helps the lover to win a lady, and it rewards the lady by the immortality it confers:

> *fortunata, meo si qua es celebrata libello!*
> *carmina erunt formae tot monumenta tuae.*

'Fortunate you, whoever you are, if you are celebrated in my volume! My songs shall be so many monuments to your beauty.'[3]

$$(3.2.17f)$$

Thus Propertius lives and writes in the comforting certainty of being a true poet, with a devoted audience during his lifetime and the promise of everlasting fame after his death. He has created art for life's sake and is ready to conclude that his is a life for art's sake.

> *at mihi quod vivo detraxerit invida turba,*
> *post obitum duplici faenore reddet Honos;*
> *omnia post obitum fingit maiora vetustas:*
> *maius ab exsequiis nomen in ora venit.*

---

[1] Cf. Tibullus 2.3.13f (of Apollo in love); Callimachus, *Ep.* 46; F. Leo, *Plautinische Forschungen*², 148, n. 2.

[2] A. L. Wheeler, *Class. Philol.* 5 (1910), 440ff; 6 (1911), 56ff.

[3] Cf. 2.5.27ff; 25.3f; Ovid, *Amores* 3.12.7.

'But what the jealous crowd has taken away from me during my lifetime, reputation will restore to me with double interest after death; an age to come, when the present shall be a distant past, magnifies everything; after the last rites, my name comes greater on to the tongues of men.'[1]

(3.1.21ff)

The unconditional praise that may be denied to him now will be more than outweighed by the immortal fame that awaits him beyond the grave.

Propertius' work is powerful in feeling and the result of great technical virtuosity. He has pushed language to extraordinary limits and charged it with meaning to the utmost degree. Most of his elegies show an abrupt method of progression, in which explanatory aids are lacking. He is a difficult poet, more difficult, I think, than Horace and Vergil; but he is not obscure on purpose, in order to mystify the reader. His obscurity is intimately connected with his sincerity and he has tried more than the other elegists to define the meaning of poetry and the role of the poet in life.

[1] Cf. Ovid, *Amores* 1.15.39ff; 3.15.20; Callimachus fr. 7.13f. H. Fränkel, *Ovid: A Poet Between Two Worlds* (1945), 33.

9

Augustan Rococo

Now soft and slow he bends the circling Round,
Now rises high upon the sprightly Bound,
Now springs aloft too swift for Mortal Sight,
Now falls unhurt from some stupendous height;
Like Proteus in a thousand Forms is seen,
Sometimes a God, sometimes a Harlequin.

> – From the *Description of a Ballet Dancer*, by MATTHEW
> TOWLE, Dancing Master in Oxford, *fl.* 1770
> (quoted by Brian Hill, *Pleasure Garden*, London,
> Rupert Hart-Davies 1956)

At the age of fifty-five, exiled, lonely and disillusioned, Ovid looks back at his life. Once more, he recaptures all the glamour and promise of his early years; once more, he tries to realize the full impact of the tragedy that changed his life.

The autobiography[1] of the last elegiac poet is quite simple and straightforward. Placed at the end of Book IV of the *Tristia*, it seals, as it were, the book and recalls the person of its author to a sympathetic audience. At the beginning, he addresses posterity. He wants future generations to know who he was. He hopes that his fame will survive his misfortune. Towards the end he is overcome once more by a sense of loss; he feels more clearly than before that now his art is nothing more than an escape from oppressive reality. But it is still his art, something unique, something to be proud of, and he knows that his personal tragedy is not the end of everything. He enjoyed his worldly

[1] G. Misch, *History of Autobiography*, I, 1 (third German ed., 1949, pp. 307ff).

success while it lasted, and now that he is disgraced, he still lives the life of the Muses.

The main part of the poem is strictly biographical. Ovid was born on 20 March 43 B.C., the year of Cicero's death. This means that he belongs already to a generation to which the Roman Republic is a mere name, not a living memory. Unlike Vergil, Horace and Propertius, who in their youth had experienced the horror of the Civil Wars, Ovid, who was twelve at the time of the battle of Actium, spent his adolescence in the comfort and security of the *Pax Augusta* and took it for granted.

He shows as little interest in politics or business as the other elegiac poets; but, unlike Tibullus and Propertius, he hardly even attempts to justify his passivity. The times have changed. Politics has now become the exclusive concern of the emperor and his cabinet. Ovid is intensely aware that he lives in one of Rome's greatest historical periods, but he refuses to have anything to do with a life of action himself. He loves Rome, the city; Rome, not Corinna, is in a sense the real protagonist of the *Amores*, and his true love. It appears as the background, the scenery, of his erotic adventures, taking the place of Tibullus' idyllic landscapes, Propertius' mythological fantasies. The streets and public buildings of the city, its boudoirs and salons, are always present in Ovid's verse.

The son of well-to-do parents, he is sent to the city, perhaps at the age of thirteen or fourteen, to receive his rhetorical training. The elder Seneca, a connoisseur of rhetoric, remembers him as an excellent student and skilful debater; but Ovid soon grew tired of the scholastic declamations he had to deliver. Like Vergil, he probably felt that the *inanes rhetorum ampullae*, the 'empty rhetorical bombast', endangered the freshness and directness of his imagination; but, unlike Vergil, who wrote painstakingly and slowly, Ovid always retained the good orator's ability to improvise:

> *sponte sua carmen numeros veniebat ad aptos,*
> *et quod temptabam dicere, versus erat.*

'Spontaneously, the poem used to fall into suitable rhythms, and whatever I attempted to say, was verse.'

(*Tristia* 4.10.25-26)

More fortunate than Propertius, who had never been in Greece, and Vergil, who went there only on the eve of his death, Ovid was sent to the eastern part of the Mediterranean world as an impressionable young man. He visited Athens, not to study philosophy, but as a tourist. From Greece, he went to Asia Minor, and on his way back to Rome, he visited Sicily. During this trip, the world of Greek mythology must have become for him a picturesque presence, a treasure-house of images.

Obeying his father's wish, he embarked on a public career and held various offices, but neither politics nor the law attracted him permanently. He preferred to live at ease and to write. As a very young man, almost an adolescent, he had found in the house of Messalla Corvinus (a friend of his family, it seems) the revelation of a thoroughly civilized way of life, where culture was not a veneer, and where literature was taken seriously.

Again, one remembers the beginnings of Propertius' career. It was only after the success of his first book of elegies that Maecenas noticed him and invited him to join his circle. To Ovid, encouragement and recognition came more smoothly. Soon he was drawn into the ambit of Messalla. Tibullus was already a member of the circle, and the presence of other elegiac poets, such as Lygdamus and Sulpicia, shows that here the love-elegy was the favourite kind of literature. Messalla must have taken an interest in the talented young Ovid, urging him to write and recite his poems. He never knew Tibullus intimately (*Trist.* 4. 10.51f) but admired his work and mourned his death (*Amores* 3.9).

His earliest poems were published in five books, one at a time, it seems with great success. In the *Amores* ('Erotic adventures', or 'Love-Poems'), Ovid shows himself the most versatile of all the elegiac poets. His ability to handle a variety of literary genres, themes and idioms is almost miraculous. His skill at finding associations and transitions where none existed, must have seemed pure magic to his contemporaries. Perhaps he simply grew bored with the medium of the erotic elegy; perhaps he felt that he had exhausted its possibilities. At any rate, he published in rapid succession a tragedy (*Medea*), imaginary love-letters of legendary men and women (*Heroides*), didactic poems (*Ars Amatoria, Remedia Amoris, Medicamina Faciei*), a poetic calendar (*Fasti*) and an enchanting set of fairy stories (*Metamorphoses*). Thanks to his amazing verbal dexterity, combined with learning and humour, he can be considered the legitimate successor of Callimachus at Rome. It is Ovid, not Propertius, who deserves the title of *Callimachus Romanus*.

Surrounded by friends and admirers, thoroughly at home in the gilded literary and social set, Ovid lives a life of comfort and contentment. He spends his days between Rome and his garden villa on the slopes between the Clodian and Flaminian ways. In his verse, he catches the rich little phrases that were passed around in the salons, playing with them like bright juggling balls.

This secure and abundant existence ended abruptly. By an edict of the Emperor – a thunderbolt out of a blue sky – the poet was banished into a remote corner of the world, Tomis (now Constanza), a town by the Black Sea. What happened to him seems like a nightmare out of a novel by Kafka. He was faced by an omnipotent, invisible accuser, charged with a crime whose exact nature he never specifies, deprived of any opportunity to defend himself. The formal accusation was based on two points: the lubricious character of the *Ars Amatoria* (although this book had been published eight years before) and an offence, whose character Ovid never discloses.

Ovid retained his citizenship and fortune, but he was exiled from the capital for the rest of his life. All his attempts to have the edict revoked failed, even after Augustus' death. A long and elaborate defence (*Tristia* II) was in vain.

Thanks to the *Tristia*, those 'mournful numbers', and the *Epistulae ex Ponto*, 'Letters from the Black Sea', those slightly monotonous laments over the slow ache of his isolation, we are well informed about the last years of his life. Among a half-civilized nation, far from the electrifying atmosphere of the city, he felt buried alive. Occasionally, he rehearses the happy past, from which an echo calls hauntingly in his ear, telling of pleasures long discarded, of hopes never realized.

Ovid died toward the end of A.D. 17, lonely and forgotten by his contemporaries, although he had symbolized a whole epoch in the poetry and social life of Rome.

He is the last great poet of the Augustan Age. More than his other works, the *Amores* represent the Augustan culture, with its superb cultivation of technique for its own sake, and its exquisite sensuousness.

Reading Ovid, one sometimes wonders whether he was frivolous by choice or through disillusionment, or, perhaps, disillusioned through frivolity. But there is not the slightest doubt that he was a great artist. We find in him a wastefulness of talent, a sense of generous overflowing of wit and imagination. There is so much talent that it can dare to squander itself even on nonsense, on luxuriant affectations, on all kinds of egomanias and capricious obsessions. Ovid's art, the art of the sentimental or ironic gesture, is unique in ancient literature.

The *Amores* are Ovid's first published work. What we have today is the second edition. Ovid himself, in a prefatory epigram, specifies that the first edition consisted of five books. He must have eliminated a considerable number of poems, guided by a self-criticism which is rarely acknowledged. His criteria were mainly aesthetic, it seems; otherwise he would hardly have kept such a poem as 3.7. All he actually says about his purpose is this:

> *levior demptis poena duobus erit.*
>
> (pref. epigr.)

The work in its new form, he implies, will be less of a 'torture'[1] to the discriminating reader. It now includes fifty elegies; fifteen each in Books I and III, twenty in Book II.

The fact that there was a double edition complicates the chronology. If we assume, for example, that 1.14, an invective against the use of cosmetics, was part of the first edition, the whole work in its original form must have been published after 16 B.C., for v. 45 refers to the Roman victory over the Sugambri, a Germanic tribe, that took place in 16/15 B.C. This, incidentally, is the latest chronological reference of the *Amores*. On the other hand, it is possible that this poem was newly added to the second edition. In this case, the first edition may have been published as early as 20 B.C.[2]

The five books of the first edition were published separately.

---

[1] *Poena* corresponds to *supplicium* in Catullus c. 14.20 (of an anthology of third-rate poets), cf. E. Reitzenstein, *Rhein. Mus.* (1935), 86f.

[2] R. P. Oliver, *Transact. and Proceed. Am. Philol. Ass.* (1945), 193.

The three books of the second edition were published as a whole.[1] The work, in its definitive form, ought to reflect an artistic development of no less than ten years; as it is, the extant poems show hardly a trace of any change in outlook or style. They could all have been written within one year.

We do not know how many elegies Ovid left out or added for the second edition. Book II has no epilogue – it may have had one in the first edition – but ends with a psychological analysis of Ovid's own complicated eroticism. The next to the last poem, 2.18, an exposition of Ovid's view of love poetry in general, has very much the character of an epilogue. Perhaps it was written for the second edition, to replace an epilogue that had been dropped. It refers already to the *Heroides* (in vv. 21ff)[2] and, perhaps, to the *Ars Amatoria* (in v. 19f).[3]

Again, 3.1, an allegorical poem on his literary plans,[4] was probably composed between the two editions. The poet seems fairly certain that he will be a successful dramatist. There must have been enough evidence to convince his readers that this promise would be fulfilled. In other words, his tragedy, *Medea*, was already known in Rome at that time.

Many of the themes of the *Amores* reappear, in a slightly different form, with a didactic twist, in the 'Art of Love'. This later work contains only one direct reference to the second edition of the *Amores* (3.343f). This does not mean that the whole *Ars Amatoria* was posterior to the second edition; its third book, where the reference is found, takes a position apart; it is addressed to female readers, while I and II are directed toward a male public. This leaves the possibility that *Ars Amatoria* I and II and the second edition of the *Amores* were published almost at the same time, in 1 B.C. or A.D. 1, followed shortly by *Ars Amatoria* III. Such a long interval between the two editions would explain conveniently the vigorous remodelling that the work underwent.[5]

[1] Th. Birt, *Philol. Wochenschr.* (1913), 1228. [2] Cf. Ovid, *Heroides* 2.

[3]   *Quod licet . . . aut artes teneri profitemur Amoris –*
                  ei mihi, praeceptis urgeor ipse meis.
But this could also refer to the *Amores*, where Ovid often assumes the role of the 'teacher of love'; cf. *Amores* 1.4.46, 2.19.34; *Trist.* 2.449f (of Tibullus); Kraus, RE 18.1921.

[4] Cf. E. Reitzenstein, op. cit. (p. 145, n. 1), 81ff; H. Fränkel, *Ovid: A Poet Between Two Worlds* (1945), 46f; Kraus, RE 18.1914.

[5] Cf. W. Eisenhut, *Gnomon* (1953), 449.

When Ovid was about eighteen years old, he began to write and recite his first poems. At that time Horace, Vergil, Tibullus and Propertius were still alive; but in spite of the competition in his own field, Ovid became known at once. His love-poems for Corinna were read all over the city; he was famous. People wanted to know who Corinna was; indeed, Ovid recalls a girl who boasted that she was Corinna.[1] But the secret was well kept – for the simple reason that the Corinna of the *Amores* never existed. It is possible that, in the first edition, she was more tangible as a person, that the couple, Ovid-Corinna, emerged more clearly as the central theme. In the second edition, however, she is a rather pale figure.[2]

It would be difficult to write the biography of Ovid's 'Corinna'. She is a composite character, a name he uses to represent the various women he has known in his youth. When he writes about 'Corinna', he is thinking of his mistress of the moment. Even so, no Roman lady would have recognized herself in Ovid's book. Among the fifty elegies of the *Amores*, only two or three seem to reflect a real experience, something that Ovid had not yet come across in his reading. So much else is 'literature' – in the best sense of the word! – and at times Corinna seems like Lesbia, Delia, Cynthia, wrapped in one. Art is to Ovid more than the imitation of life; it is a constant and conscious competition with famous models from Homer to the present.

In later years, Ovid writes in defence of his erotic poetry:

vita verecunda est, Musa iocosa mea.

'My life is chaste, only my Muse is frivolous.'

(*Tristia* 2.354)[3]

It is difficult to reconcile this statement with certain situations of the *Amores*, but they should not be taken too literally. All that matters to Ovid is the variety of moods and situations. There is a very slender thread of real events, and a great deal of imagination and purely literary echoes. On the whole, this kind of love-poetry aims at the general, not the individual. Every Roman

[1] Cf. *Amores* 2.17.29f; Kraus, RE 18.1914. Cf. below, p. 167, n.1.

[2] R. Harder and W. Marg, *Ovidi Amores* (Heimeran 1956), 151.

[3] Cf. Catullus 16.5, *nam castum esse decet pium poetam Ipsum, versiculos nihil necessest*; Martial 1.4.8, *lasciva est nobis pagina, vita proba est.*

youth who read the *Amores* should discover much of his own experience in the book.

When Ovid began to compose his first erotic elegies, the masterpieces of the genre had already been written. To compete with Catullus, Tibullus and Propertius, to say something new, to explore unknown states of the soul, was an almost impossible task. Any other poet than Ovid would have failed at it.

Tibullus' rightful domain was the Italian countryside, the simplicity of bucolic life. Propertius had breathed new life into the world of the myth. What area of experience was left to Ovid that he could claim as his own?

Like Propertius, he is attracted by the psychological complications of a love-relationship. Unlike the Umbrian poet, he does not attempt to resolve these problems, but passes them over with a joke, an ironic remark. This difference is a matter of artistic temperament. Ovid refuses to take life seriously; anything that cannot be described elegantly is not worth talking about. Reason finally triumphs over the detours of passion.

He relies much more on purely 'literary' procedures than his predecessors. His technique and imagery are Alexandrian, and so is much of the material he has adapted. He has naturally read an enormous amount of Greek poetry; at the same time, he takes advantage of the work of his Latin predecessors. He is the first Roman poet who is clearly aware of the fact that Roman literature has come into its own and can henceforth renew itself from its own resources.

It could not be his intention to preserve the time-honoured modes of thought and expression, the worn-out conceits and the slightly dusty coinages of the *sermo amatorius*, the 'language of love'. Although his view of life may be one-sided, he has, in feeling and language, expressed something nearer the ever-changing experience of reality than a previous generation could.

We have said that he concentrates primarily on technique, on formal patterns of composition and verse-making. This does not mean that he is satisfied with the formal treatment of emotional themes. On the contrary, he is interested in people and their feelings and he has a remarkable psychological understanding of women. Even his most frivolous work, the 'Art of Love', clearly shows his kind and considerate nature.

Ovid's *Amores* are not a lyrical novel. The order of situations and events, the arrangement of the poems within the books, is not dictated by chronology or dramatic effect. Certain simple outlines are visible, but how much do they add to the understanding of the single poem?

Book I shows the love-affair in its beginnings. He falls in love (1.2), he swears to be faithful (1.3), he fights against initial difficulties (4, 6, 10, 12), he enjoys the pleasures of one of their first clandestine meetings (5), he has his first quarrel and regrets it bitterly afterwards (7).

In Book II, the poet is already sure of Corinna's love. Now he is looking for new conquests; he has less illusions about his ability to remain faithful:

> centum sunt causae cur ego semper amem.

'there are a hundred reasons for me to be always in love.'
(2.4.10)

He is still jealous of Corinna, but would not mind an adventure with another woman, if she is attractive (2), nor for that matter, with Corinna's maid (7 and 8), if she is willing.

Book III, finally, contains poems that might have been written during any phase of Ovid's relationship with Corinna (or any other woman). There is not even the suggestion of a biographical pattern. As a whole, it is a book of reprobation and dissatisfaction. The mood of its elegies ranges from resignation, sometimes playful, often bitter (3, 11) to genuine annoyance (7) and heart-felt regret (9, on the death of Tibullus).

Another principle of arrangement, much more significant, runs through the whole collection: it is the principle of *variatio*, which seems to underlie to Hellenistic and Roman books of poetry. It means that similar poems are often separated from each other, sometimes even placed in different books. A favourite theme of the erotic elegy, for example, the interest of the beloved in money and gifts, is treated from two different points of view. She wants gifts (1.10); she prefers a wealthier rival (3.8). The account of their first meeting (1.5) corresponds to the triumphant poem 2.12, 'she is mine'.

The same theme is occasionally treated in an antithetical

157

manner. In 1.3, Ovid affirms: 'You are the only one'; in 2.4, he admits: 'They all attract me.' Two elegies, 1.4 and 2.5, deal with the same situation (a banquet) and the same motif (the triangle), but from an entirely different point of view; the villain has now become the victim.

Sometimes, two successive poems have the same theme and achieve, as a group, an effect which is doubtless intended by the poet. He sends a passionate letter to a lady (1.11); the letter comes back with a refusal (1.12). Corinna is pregnant (2.13); she has an abortion (2.14). Ovid has a conversation with the eunuch, Bagoas (2.2 and 3), and a love-affair with Corinna's maid (2.7 and 8).

Through all these procedures (contrast, correspondence, analogy, association), Ovid creates the impression of variety. Each poem can be read and enjoyed as a unity, but it also derives a special effect from its place within the whole collection. From those colourful vicissitudes, the poet emerges as the protagonist, working tirelessly from episode to episode, holding up to the light the same precious materials.

There is also a great wealth of literary forms, all of which Ovid handles with equal facility. We find highly technical pieces of rhetoric, such as 3.4, an appeal to the *vir* (husband or friend),[1] who guards Corinna jealously. We find funeral elegies, such as 2.6, on the death of Corinna's parrot, and 3.9, on the death of the poet Tibullus. There is a so-called προπεμπτικόν, a 'bon-voyage' poem (2.11), and a παρακλαυσίθυρον, the locked-out lover's serenade (1.6). The third book, finally, contains several mythological and narrative poems, for example, 3.6, the catalogue of rivers in love, a sort of preview of the *Metamorphoses*.

The structure of the Ovidian elegy is clear and straightforward. The single poem usually deals with one well-defined topic. Unlike Tibullus, Ovid does not rely on the suggestiveness of mood and the delicacy of the verbal music to bind the whole together. He avoids the abrupt, passionate transitions of Propertius.

---

[1] A. D. Nock, in his commentary to 'Magical Texts from a Bilingual Papyrus', *Proceedings of the British Academy* 17 (1931), p. 281, comments on the significance of *vir* in Latin love-poetry: '. . . *vir* may well be . . . the lover in possession . . .' (cf. Catullus c. 68.135ff, 83.1; Tibullus 1.2.21, 6.8; Ovid, *Ars Amatoria* 1.579). He adds that, in Ovid's time, concubinage (e.g. with a freedwoman) was a relationship almost as fixed as marriage.

From his careful rhetorical training, Ovid has retained the ability to handle his material as if he were pleading a case. If the theme involves an antithesis, it is neatly divided into two parts, such as the *odi et amo*, 'I love and I hate' of 3.11.

The *propositio*, or thesis, is often stated right at the beginning, then developed methodically, each distich usually representing a step forward in a logical progression. Frequently, the poems end in an epigram or dismiss the reader with a witty *tour de force*.

One should not overstate the intellectual character of the Ovidian love-elegy. These poems are not mere expansions or amplifications of Greek epigrams. Ovid is a poet of Order rather than Adventure, and his images unfold as elegantly as the variations of a Mozart sonata. He likes to set himself a problem and then treat it exhaustively, fitting in all the elements provided by mythology and literary history.

But is it not the very abundance of his ideas that forces him to be so methodical? His universal interests and omnivorous culture had to be disciplined. In his best poems, the argumentation gently underlines the mood of the situation. A well-known example is 1.13, a poem whose charm consists in the contrast between the background and the colours that are superimposed. But there is also a subtle relationship between the atmosphere of dawn and the feeling of weariness that comes with waking up in a large city.

One often wonders whether Ovid was capable of genuine passion. We have his own confession

> *molle Cupidineis nec inexpugnabile telis*
> *cor mihi . . .*

'my heart was ever soft and easy to be conquered by the darts of Cupid . . .'

(Tristia 4.10.65f)

The typical situations of the *Amores* suggest that Ovid was tender and sentimental in anticipation and remembrance, but often clumsy and impatient in action. He speaks of sex frankly, even boldly, but so did Catullus and Horace before him. As a lover, he seems rather more courteous and delicate than, for example, Propertius. At times, he even betrays a certain *naïveté*. No wonder that later, during the Middle Ages (and especially during the twelfth century), Ovid was the favourite author of a chivalrous society.

For Ovid, love is more than a mere fulfilment of man's physical desires. It includes a wide range of feelings, from quiet affection to violent passion.

> *a, nimium volui — tantum patiatur amari;*
> *audierit nostras tot Cytherea preces!*
>
> *(Amores* 1.3.3-4; cf. 3.2.57)

Like Tibullus and Propertius, Ovid is a believer in the gospel of romantic love. It is an irrational force, difficult to describe and to control. He calls himself a 'slave of love', a 'soldier of love'; he speaks of his own 'worthlessness', but these confessions are partly elegiac convention, partly self-irony. Catullus suffers, and we believe him, but when Ovid goes on and on, telling us how he suffers, we have our doubts.

In many respects, the *Amores* anticipate the 'Art of Love'. In both works, he does not only want to entertain but tries to understand love as a phenomenon, to explore the psychology of the lover. Ovid is interested in the typical rather than in the individual, irrecoverable aspects of each experience. In the *Amores*, each poem has its own mood, and the point of view changes from situation to situation. He praises *fides*, 'faith', and *pudor* ,'modesty', in 1.3, but in other poems, he implies that these ideals have only a relative value.

Before we study a few more aspects of Ovid's mind and style, we should interpret at least one elegy as a whole. So much of his art consists in the structure, in surprising transitions, in unexpected turns of the thought, in a brilliantly polished detail here and there, that it can only be described concretely in the context of the poem itself.

One of the poems in which the natural blend of fantasy and flesh-and-blood, that is characteristic of all of Ovid's poetry, is most successful, is the account of his first secret *rendez-vous* with Corinna, 1.5. In this elegy, the poet introduces himself to his readers as a connoisseur of love, a casual and mildly cynical man-about-town. He introduces Corinna, the eternal mistress, lush, languid, yet, as he flatters himself, *verecunda*.

The whole poem is a little masterpiece, far more convincing

than the treatments of the same motif in the Greek Anthology.[1]
Ovid knew the literary models with whom he competed well
enough; indeed, he is so sure of himself that he invites comparison. We do not know when Ovid wrote this poem, but the date
is irrelevant. All the experiences Ovid was ever going to have,
he seems to have had as a very young man; all the emotions he
was ever going to feel, he seems to have felt already and measured
against the capacity of his art to express them.

The secret of this art lies in the elegance and smoothness with
which he handles the elegiac form. Everything he has to say
appears quite natural, quite uncomplicated. Under the polished
surface, no conflict seems to exist; in the realm of Ovid's art,
there is no discord between the intellect and the senses. He loves
the body and the soul.

Our poem is typical in more than one way for much of Ovid's
erotic poetry. Corinna is depicted as beauty personified, as a
living, breathing, stirring presence. Love is seen as pleasure and
fulfilment, not as longing and unrequited desire. This is not an
adolescent's attitude; Ovid is experienced enough to know that
happiness is only possible within narrow limits. One brief moment
of rapture is all that counts, and he refuses to cloud that moment
by any thoughts of parting.

We find the opposite type of love in Tibullus – a romantic
day-dream, a longing without fulfilment; or in Lygdamus – a kind
of sentimental resignation. In those two poets of Messalla's circle,
love is an emotion which affects only a part of the soul, not the
whole personality.

Ovid's art is by no means all play and frivolity. At times, there
is a deep seriousness under the smiling mask. He is dedicated to
a serene cult of the senses, of beauty and its visible incarnation
here and now. Dissatisfied with the fickleness of *Tyche*, 'Chance',
he creates a world in which everything happens more smoothly
and more intensely.

This splendid private world shines in Ovid's love-poems with
the particular finality that high technique can give. Did he expect
Corinna to visit him on that afternoon? He must have been

[1] Cf. Philodem. 5.4 Anth .Pal. and 132. Here Ovid could have found the two
main elements of his poem: (1) the description of Corinna's beauty; (2) the elegant
formula 'who does not know the rest?' (v. 25).

prepared for her visit, for he took great care to create the right illumination:

> *illa verecundis lux est praebenda puellis,*
> *qua timidus latebras speret habere pudor.*

'That kind of light must be offered to nice girls, such a light as their modesty may hope to find a hiding-place in.'

(v. 7-8)

In the last line, Ovid congratulates himself on the pleasant afternoon he has spent. He gives the impression that this conquest did not cost him a great effort. Throughout the love-scene, he is not too active; the mood of the poem is carried by the descriptive passages. There is little need for violent action. Once he has torn away her tunic –

> *deripui tunicam . . .*

Corinna is 'overcome by her own betrayal' (v. 16). After the breathless praise of her beautiful body, which is now exposed, he utters a laconic sentence:

> *cetera quis nescit?*

'The rest, who does not know?'

(v. 25)

thus avoiding any realism that might endanger the equilibrium of the whole. Far from being lascivious for the sake of lasciviousness, Ovid believes in a certain restraint.

The tone and the imagery of the poem are influenced by Hellenistic poetry. The details of the scenery, the description of Corinna's beauty, the swift transitions – all this reveals the Alexandrian technique. The room is compared to a grove, and its well-calculated illumination to the natural light of the dawn (v. 4-6). Ovid is sparing in the use of mythological examples; he adds only one picturesque touch, at Corinna's triumphant entrance, comparing her to Semiramis and, in the same breath, to Lais.

Nevertheless, this is a thoroughly Roman poem.[1] It sets a

[1] The initial situation must have been familiar to any Roman reader. Ovid closes one of the shutters at his window and leaves the other open (see Kiessling-Heinze

pattern and suggests possibilities of conduct beyond the individual experience. This distinguishes it from comparable Greek poems, such as *Anth. Pal.* 5.56, whose author, Dioscorides, the last of the great Alexandrian epigrammatists, has written a number of short, spirited love-poems. This portrait of a very seductive girl might have furnished Ovid with some of the colours for the description of Corinna. In any event, it is characteristic of a good deal of Hellenistic love-poetry. If Ovid was not acquainted with this very poem, he had certainly read a great many similar ones.

'They drive me mad with passion, those rose-coloured lips of various discourse, soul-melting portals of a nectareous mouth, and the eyes flashing under thick brows, nets and traps of my heart, and those milky, well-matched, lovely, shapely breasts, more delightful than any rosebud. But why am I pointing out bones to dogs? Midas' reeds are witnesses of (the peril of) impudent loquacity.'

(Anth. Pal. 5.56)

In a description of the same length (eight lines), Dioscorides has no less than ten epithets, Ovid only five, all of them sober and restrained: *apta premi*, 'suited for caress'; *castigato*, 'firm'; *iuvenale*, 'youthful'; *laudabile*, 'worthy of praise'; *nudam*, 'naked'. The luxuriant visual impressions of the Greek poet have yielded to tactile sensations and a kind of over-all intellectual appreciation.

One should keep in mind that the epigram, as an art-form, aims at a different effect and requires a technique different from that of the elegy. The situation as such is of little interest. What matters is the unexpected twist at the end – a proverb, or a mythological allusion.

---

on Horace c. 1.25.1). He lies down on the couch to have his *meridiatio*, 'mid-day siesta'. The mood he was in is described in a much more realistic manner by Catullus, c. 32. Professor Nock has drawn my attention to a similar description of female beauty, on a popular level, in the curious epitaph of Allia Potestas, from Rome (Via Salaria, third or fourth century A.D.), *Carm. Lat. Epigr.* 1988 (vol. III, ed. Buecheler-Lommatzsch). This woman, whose praises assume mythical dimensions (her thighs are compared to those of Atalante, her fatal charms to those of Helen of Troy . . . and what limbs! *levia membra tulit, pilus illi quaesitus ubique*) lived in happy union with two men whose common interest in her brought them as close to each other as Orestes and Pylades had been. The epitaph reveals a prurience that is disarmingly naïve.

163

The technique of the enumeration, the short, breathless sentences, the rapt exclamations over so much beauty – all this Ovid could have learned from Dioscorides. But there is one great difference. The epigram captures a mood, adds a few casual observations, suggests a conventional feeling, while the elegy relates any such feelings or thoughts to a larger context. It is impossible to understand Ovid's poem as a mere rhetorical amplification of a Greek epigram. Two or three new images and a paradoxical thought are not sufficient to transform an epigram into an elegy.

Ovid plays ingeniously with the traditional themes, but at the same time brings them to life. The only touch of colour in Ovid's poem is 'white' (v. 10), of Corinna's neck. He refuses to pour out a blinding wealth of visual impressions. In the chiaroscuro of a quiet room, on a hot afternoon in the south, colours and outlines blend into each other. To see something in this semi-darkness, means to be close enough to touch it:

> *quos umeros, quales vidi tetigique lacertos . . .*

'what shoulders, what arms did I see – and touch!'

(v. 19)

Ovid's versatility has been interpreted as lack of character, his command of the form as neglect of the substance. To realize how unconventional he is, to admire the freshness of his talent, we should read every poem of his in the light of parallel texts. One more example must suffice. In an elegy more than twice as long as Ovid's, Propertius (2.15) has told a similar story. It may be worth our while to study a particular theme in its transition from epigrammatic to elegiac treatment.

Propertius' poem begins with the rapt exclamations which we have already found in Dioscorides, but they are not caused by anything he sees or grasps. On the contrary, they sum up his exaltation at the remembrance of an almost painfully happy experience. He is so carried away that he does not take time to describe the situation. Ovid, on the other hand, keeps the narrative section of his poem neatly separated from the one short emotional outburst. For this reason, Propertius' elegy may seem more satisfactory as a poem than Ovid's. The confusion of sights and sounds, the vague outlines visible in the semi-darkness, the whispering excitement that has magically transformed the room – all this cannot be conveyed in neat portions of narrative. Propertius is carried away by his memories; past and present blend into one. Ovid writes more leisurely; he has the ability to experience romantic emotions and, half an hour later, regard them with detachment.

Ultimately, this difference is a matter of artistic temperament. There are poets who dwell with a fervent intensity upon experience as it is offered to them, not for the lessons it can give, but for what it is in itself. Catullus and Propertius belong to this class. Ovid's art is too rational and, in spite of his facility, too self-disciplined to permit such an abandon.

10

The Necessity of Self-Deception

Ovid . . . is the gayest and most playful of Latin writers. Perhaps he has not more humour than Apuleius, but he did not feel it necessary to invent a new language; he was content to write Latin. No one wrote with more grace; no one can be read with more ease . . . [but] . . . there are no undertones, no harmonics, about Ovid's work; it is all on the surface. . . .

> — T. R. GLOVER, in *The Cambridge Ancient History*, vol. 10 (1934), p. 533

The elegiac tradition seems to require that the poet be faithful to the same woman throughout the same book of poetry. If we discount the Marathus-episode, Tibullus was in love with Delia throughout Book I, and with Nemesis throughout Book II. Propertius' love for Cynthia is unswerving, at least in the *Monobiblos*. This custom was probably inherited from the archaic and post-classical Greek elegy; it is sufficient to recall Mimnermus' *Nanno* and Antimachus' *Lyde*, books which had as their title the name of the poet's wife or mistress.

Propertius once objects to the fickleness of his friend Gallus (1.13). In the second book, however, he finds himself in Gallus' position (2.22.1ff). Ovid, of course, has to go one step further. What seems to be the mood of a moment in Propertius becomes an elaborate dialectic system, justified as such in his elegy 2.4.

The personality of the poet asserts itself against the rules of tradition. This was possible partly because Corinna, though she may have been a real person, was also a label conveniently attached to Ovid's various love-affairs, day-dreams and rhetorical exercises. He needed this fiction to transform the erotic themes of Alexandrian poetry into personal experience. The legendary heroines who love and offer and spin their intrigues in such works as Parthenius'

'Erotic Adventures' (only an extract from Hellenistic poems) are very pale and synthetic indeed. Ovid creates Corinna as if she were a character in a play; she has a certain individuality, but she may have been much less fascinating in real life.[1]

2.4 is one of Ovid's more original creations. True, it displays an unusual wealth of Hellenistic themes, but Ovid wanted to show that he could use these motifs in a new way. They all serve as illustrations of his cherished weakness – his appetite for erotic adventure.

> *Denique quas tota quisquam probet urbe puellas,*
> *noster in has omnis ambitiosus amor.*

'Finally, whatever girls anyone could praise in the whole city – my love is a candidate for the favours of them all.'

(v. 47f)

The whole poem is an elegant specimen of self-analysis. Ovid pretends to be puzzled by his own nature and he even seems to regret his weakness, though he has no intention of fighting it.

A brief analysis will show the main outlines. The introduction includes the lines 1-8. Ovid begins with an admission of his guilt. He does not even try to defend himself – an ingenious move, for the rest of the poem, as we shall see, is nothing but a rationalization of his weakness. This is by far the most significant part of the elegy. What follows is little more than an enumeration of the different kinds of beauties that appeal to Ovid, and he easily achieves new triumphs in the Hellenistic technique of catalogue-poetry. But the introduction tells us more about his personality.

Ovid knows that there is a conflict between the rational and the irrational element in his soul. This is not a new discovery. For the first time in ancient literature, Euripides' *Medea* expressed the sense of two conflicting forces within the human soul:

'I know what evil I am about to do, but my passion is stronger than my knowledge of what is best.'

(Euripides, *Medea*, vv. 1078f)[2]

---

[1] Nobody in Rome knew who she was; *Amores* 2.17.29, *novi aliquam quae se circumferat esse Corinnam*; cf. *Ars Amatoria* 3.538; *Tristia* 4.10.60; Kraus, RE 18.1914.

[2] I owe this comparison (and the translation from Euripides' *Medea*) to D. W. Lucas, *The Greek Tragic Poets* (1952), 162.

No other ancient poet has expressed this conflict more compellingly than Catullus in his distich, *Odi et amo*. It is natural that Catullus' epigram comes to Ovid's mind:

> *Odi, nec possum, cupiens, non esse quod odi;*
> *heu, quam quae studeas ponere ferre grave est.*

'I hate what I am; and yet, for all my striving, I can only be what I hate. Ah, how hard it is to bear the burden you long to lay aside.'

(vv. 5-6)

Ovid's variation of Catullus' poem is skilful enough. He repeats the word *odi* at the beginning and end of the hexameter to emphasize the vicious circle in which he is caught. The antithesis of *ponere*, 'to lay aside', and *ferre*, 'to bear', is made more striking by the juxtaposition of the contrasting terms. But there is one important difference: In Ovid the conflict is not felt as tragic. A person who is torn between two decisions, he seems to imply, is not necessarily weak or immoral. Only sensitive and imaginative persons ever feel this conflict at all. Medea is a strong woman, stronger than Jason, her antagonist. She stands above the dramatic situation, outside society and the rules which society has established. Because of her superior intelligence and sensitivity she has the urge to explore herself, to find out what *makes* her different. Catullus, unable to cope with the conventions of everyday life, was haunted by the same desire. For Ovid the issue had lost its urgency. He was exclusively interested in the formal treatment of an emotional theme. He puts his genius into his art, not into his life.

The first distich after the introduction contains the *propositio*, the 'theme':

> *Non est certa meos quae forma invitet amores:*
> *centum sunt causae, cur ego semper amem.*

'There is no definite kind of beauty that stimulates my love – there are a hundred reasons for me to be always in love.'

(v. 9f)

After the promises of eternal devotion to Corinna in Book I, this comes as a surprise. Which is the true Ovid, the faithful lover of 1.3, or the scoundrel of 2.4? Neither, it seems; for both his tender devotion and his cynical frankness are literary attitudes. It is doubtful whether Ovid at all times really wants to know the truth about himself. What matters to him is the believable presentation of a paradoxical, unconventional theme or situation.

Throughout this poem Ovid poses as a kind of rebel against society and middle-class morality. But his rebellion is in turn becalmed by convention and, at the end, appears quite harmless. He has not forgotten the rhetorical precepts he learned as a young man. He knows that he needs the sympathy of his audience to make his case convincing.

For this reason he makes it quite clear he did not feel too comfortable in the role of the snob. He sounds contrite, ashamed of himself; his confession has a note of *naïveté* that is rather refreshing and disarming, as if he felt sorry for his wickedness. Actually it is all a game with pretences, a highly ironical game that questions the accepted values without intending to overthrow them.

In a long list of contrasting portraits of women (vv. 11ff) Ovid unfolds his main thesis. He draws a series of vignettes, capturing in each case the characteristic detail. The various types of girls who appeal to him are presented in a logical order; first, those who charm him by their character (vv. 11-16); then the girls whose talents or achievements he admires (vv. 17-30); and finally, those who attract him physically (vv. 33-48).

He begins with the shy girl (vv. 11-12) and a description of her alluring coyness. His appreciation of modesty in a woman is probably quite genuine. In another poem (3.6.67f), Ilia, a Roman heroine, is introduced in very similar terms. The procuress in 1.8 knows how irresistible modesty is; she advises Corinna to cast her eyes down modestly while she quickly appraises the gifts offered to her by her lover. Throughout this poem he praises faith and loyalty as the highest values. This preaching tone is characteristic of Book I, while the following books are more disillusioned in their outlook.

Continuing his enumeration, he admits that the *puella procax*, the 'provocative girl', attracts him just as much. He has in mind the 'experienced' city-girl (*non rustica*, v. 13); Corinna's maid-servant, Cypassis, is an example of this type (2.8.3). In the 'Remedies of Love' (v. 329f) Ovid twists the same motif to serve a different purpose. Again, he starts from the premise that defects are close to virtues. If you love a girl, he says in the later work, because she is 'experienced', call her 'forward' and you will learn to dislike her. Ovid is fond of these quips and quiddities; if they were worth tossing off once, they were worth tossing off again; the truth is whatever suits his thesis.

If a girl is neither shy nor provocative, but austere (*aspera*, v. 15), she represents a different kind of challenge. It will be a pleasure to break her resistance. The technique that must be applied is discussed elaborately in the 'Art of Love' (2.177ff). Here again Ovid has resumed a theme of his earlier love-poetry and treated it in a didactic manner.

A thoroughly cultivated woman (v. 17) appeals to his vanity as an author. She is able to appreciate his art. An uneducated girl, on the other hand, has a charm of her own (v. 18). Simplicity is one of the ancient Roman virtues (*Ars Amatoria* 3.113). Naturally she must be approached in a different way (*Ars Amatoria* 1.767).

These comparisons between Ovid's love poems and his technical treatises could be carried further. Almost every line of 2.4 has its analogies in Ovid's later works. Instead of studying these parallels it might be useful for a moment to place 2.4 next to 2.10, a poem which bears an obvious resemblance to it. The situation of the poet who is torn between two loves is a popular topic of the Hellenistic erotic epigram.[1] In *Amores* 2.10 Ovid has treated it in the more heavy-handed, speculative Propertian manner.

Some critics have said that this poem lacks real experience. Indeed, it seems to hang somewhat in the air. Ovid reaches the conclusion that it is better to be caught in a conflict between two loves than not to love at all. This leads up to one of the favourite propositions[2] of all elegiac poets, from Mimnermus to Ovid. They all agree that only a life of love is worth living. As a solution of the poet's initial dilemma this is not very convincing.

2.10 seems like a preparatory sketch of 2.4. The situation is simpler; there are only two girls instead of an infinite number of

[1] Cf. Philodemus, *Anth. Pal.* 12.173; Polystratus, *Anth. Pal.* 12.91; anon., *Anth. Pal.* 12.88.

[2] Cf. Mimnermus, fr. 1D; Alpheius of Mytilene, *Anth. Pal.* 12.18; E. Burck, *Hermes* (1952), 173, n. 1; 190.

temptations, but this distinction is irrelevant. In both poems the conflict is an intellectual game. Ovid sees reality sometimes through a veil or a coloured mist of mythological lore and literary tradition. Leda is a brunette to him; Aurora a blonde:

> omnibus historiis se meus aptat amor,

> 'my love adapts itself to all the stories.'

(2.4.44)

This line is characteristic of the role that mythology plays in Ovid's work. In Catullus such allusions were largely intended as an ornament. In Propertius they helped to objectify actual experience. In Ovid they act perhaps as a drug to stimulate the jaded appetites of an over-refined public, unless he offers them simply as specimens of his vast erudition. But his erudition is almost a way of looking at things.

As with every artist who is his own favourite sitter, Ovid's subject never changes; yet each elegy is a fresh start and often has its surprises. As 2.10 simplifies the thesis of 2.4, so 2.7 contradicts it. Here Ovid claims that he never even looks at another woman. With an undertone of hurt dignity he defends himself against Corinna's jealousy:

> 'Am I, then, to stand trial on new complaints for ever?'

(2.7.1)

This apology follows right after the admission of guilt in 2.4 and precedes another poem, 2.8, which proves so clearly that Ovid lies. In spite of his protest he enjoys being with Corinna's maid-servant; what 2.8 admits in one particular case, 2.4 states as a general principle. Like the protagonist of a play he confesses to the audience what he denies to the leading heroine.

Still the whole theme of guilt and confession, jealousy and self-defence, has a strong fascination for him. In the 'Art of Love' (2.641-702) he proves with a host of examples that 'no woman should be reproached with her own faults'. Label the fault with a nice name and it becomes a virtue. This is an old rhetorical precept, recommended by Aristotle and Quintilian and explored from a philosophical point of view by Plato and Lucretius.[1] While

---

[1] Plato, *Rep.* 474D/E; Aristotle, *Rhet.* 1.9, p. 1367A; Lucretius 4.1160ff; Quintilian 3.7.25.

Ovid poses, in 2.4, as a victim of this truth, he turns it to practical advantage in his 'Art of Love'. Witty and gay, with a wonderful sense of the absurd, he indulges there his natural taste for sophistic tricks. We can only admire this magical talent which turns white into black and vice versa.

Perhaps we should pause here for a moment to trace the history of this motif in erotic poetry. It may be rewarding to observe its transformation from a philosophical (and rhetorical) commonplace into a *topos* of the love-elegy.

It appears for the first time in erotic poetry in a short elegy of the Hellenistic poet, Rhianus (latter part of the third century B.C.). This little-known writer celebrates the charms of various boys whom he calls by their names (*Anth. Pal.* 12.93): Theodorus, Philocles, Leptines. All these boys are handsome, each in his own way. They are altogether 'a labyrinth with no exit' (v. 1) – incidentally the only original line in the whole poem.

After Rhianus, the dilemma of the poet torn between several equally attractive boys (or girls) becomes one of the more popular themes of Greek epigrammatic poetry. Strato (*Anth. Pal.* 12.5) admits that he likes blond and dark boys, boys with bright and dark eyes. Nicarchus (*Anth. Pal.* 5.38) declares that he is fond of tall women, no matter whether they are old or young.

None of these poets has Ovid's blend of *naïveté* and irony; none of their epigrams has achieved the consistent elegance of his imagery and the penetrating intelligence of his style.

Ovid has exhausted his topic in forty-eight lines, keeping strictly to the point, neatly subordinating arguments and examples to general propositions, re-phrasing his conclusions, arranging his thoughts like a well-ordered phalanx. Propertius (2.22A), in a poem of almost equal length (forty-two lines) loses himself in three different topics before he returns to the main point.

But Ovid's poem is not all polished surface and bland persuasion. He has explored more seriously the root of an almost metaphysical longing. The desire which he describes is similar to an endless movement, an ever new beginning or, perhaps, a series of new beginnings, where each is more startlingly new than the previous one. This is not necessarily a tragic situation. The tragedy of Ovid is that of Don Juan. Both are fascinated by the magic of numbers. With admirable boldness they accept quantity and number as values *per se*. To cumulate experience upon experience, to make the immeasurable measurable, this is their ambition. Ovid desires in order to desire, but his desire grasps its object with self-abandon and without any afterthoughts. It is a carefree feeling which reveals a certain artistic innocence; for once, the 'chaste life' and the 'frivolous Muse' are working, not against, but with each other.

Ovid is the eternal *charmeur* who enjoys intensely the passion which he inspires but also enters wholeheartedly into the game of courtship and flirtation. His moods are the moods of desire and they have the spontaneity, the youth, the ardour, and the exuberant gaiety of a desire that always fulfils itself. In life, the unexpected always seems to happen, and for Ovid, reality is paradoxical.

He is usually described as the representative of a society for whom nothing was important but pleasure and witty talk about pleasure. This is an over-simplification. Very often we find in Ovid's poetry a sense of human suffering that reminds us of Sappho or Catullus or Vergil. Some of his best passages seem to show that he is a moralist at heart.

3.14 is one of these elegies. Its composition is simple and straightforward. The first two distichs state the theme in a symmetrical arrangement of thesis and antithesis:

> *non ego, ne pecces, cum sis formosa, recuso,*
> *sed ne sit misero scire necesse mihi;*
> *nec te nostra iubet fieri censura pudicam,*
> *sed tamen ut temptes dissimulare rogat.*

'I do not ask you not to sin – you are too beautiful; but let it not be necessary for me to know it. I am not pretending to be a censor, asking you to become chaste; but you might at least try to be discreet.'

In the next two lines (v. 5f) the poet explains the nature of her *peccatum*, 'sin'[1]; it is not the act itself but the rumours it

---

[1] The concept of *peccatum* plays a great role in Ovid's thought. In the *Tristia* and *Epistulae ex Ponto*, he rehearses endlessly the catastrophe that struck him in A.D. 8, but already in his early love-elegies he is intensely concerned with the question of

provokes, the humiliation it implies, that constitute her guilt. Indeed, this is more than *peccatum*; it is *furor*, 'madness' (vv. 7-14). He is ready to believe in her innocence, to cherish the thinnest illusion as long as she does not wilfully destroy it.

The definition of Corinna's 'sin' calls for a definition of its opposite, *pudor*, 'modesty'. It is a very liberal concept of *pudor* that Ovid proposes in the next seven distichs (vv. 15-28), in the typical discursive manner of his elegy, with frequent repetitions of the key-term. These fine-spun, pseudo-moral or even pseudo-legal distinctions are followed by a brief restatement of the theme (vv. 29-30). At the same time, Ovid proposes to make a fresh start in their relationship. Henceforth it will be based on *stulta credulitas*, 'foolish trust' (v. 30).

After once more rehearsing the evidence against her, Ovid builds up toward the climax of his poem in a highly emotional account of his tortures:

> *mens abit et morior quotiens peccasse fateris,*
> *   perque meos artus frigida gutta fluit.*
> *tunc amo, tunc odi frustra quod amare necesse est;*
> *   tunc ego, sed tecum, mortuus esse velim!*

'My mind fails me and I swoon each time you admit your guilt, and through my limbs the blood runs cold. In such a moment I love you, in such a moment I try in vain to hate what I am forced to love; in such a moment, I wish I were dead – but dead with you!'

(vv. 37-40)

The last part marks a return to the calmer mood of the beginning; the poet has now learned to see his conflict from a certain distance. He plays in an experimental way with some of the

---

personal guilt, of remorse, and forgiveness. *Peccatum* in Ovid is 'sin as trespassing'; *peccare*, originally 'to stumble', then 'to commit a mistake', hence 'to sin', but without any Christian connotation. The concept of redemption from a state of sinfulness is absent from Ovid. Under the influence of Greek moral thought *peccatum* had, long before Ovid, become identical with *culpa*, 'guilt as fact' (first in Terence, then in Cicero). 'Ovid', as Professor Nock writes (*Journ. Rom. Stud.* 45 (1955), 239, in his notice of A. E. Wilhelm-Hooijbergh, *Peccatum: Sin and Guilt in Ancient Rome*, Diss. Utrecht), '. . . had a personal preoccupation with guilt in its various gradations, but moralizing was in the tradition of Latin love poetry from Catullus 76 onwards, as contrasted with *Anth. Pal.* V.'

concepts he has thrown into the discussion. To show how deep his love is, he leads his own policy of non-interference *ad absurdum*, and his quiet resignation contrasts effectively with this bizarre resolution (vv. 41-50).

Ovid is, at times, a moralist, and at times a psychologist, and he has a tendency to lecture. But in this elegy he reveals an exceptional breadth of vision, a passionate acceptance of life, life in all its aspects, the ugly and harsh as well as the lovely and pleasurable. For once he has abandoned the pose of the dandy who is perpetually infatuated with himself and his views. He has given up the role of the detached and amused observer of life who has gratified every wish and found every gratification equally tiring and transitory.

To be in love, to make love, is for Ovid a natural activity, provided that it leads to mutual pleasure. It is unnatural, however, to seek in love a purely selfish satisfaction. This aberration, according to Ovid, comes close to what the Greek tragic poets called *hubris*. Ovid interprets it as the symptom of a decadent society which has forgotten the art of enjoying pleasures for their own sake. Means have become ends and love has become a game to relieve the boredom of shallow lives.

Ovid's answer to these perversions is no less symptomatic, although he does not seem to be aware of it. His resolution to turn his head the other way, to believe Corinna's explanations more than his own eyes – all this seems at least as unnatural as the attitude he claims to abhor. By a desperate dialectical effort he tries to give new meaning to a futile and false practice, because he wants to prove to himself that faith and loyalty – in an agonized and distorted form, to be sure – are still possible in an age of suspicion and suave deceit.

Perhaps I am not fair to Ovid. He knows the truth, but *accepts* it. This is not unnatural; it is the reaction of a man who dislikes his girl's infidelity, but prefers to pretend he does not know about it. If he were in love, he would not behave like this. But he wants to go on enjoying her occasional favours; hence he tries to pretend to himself that he does not care about her feelings. The only alternative, he knows, is to lose her.

There is an element of self-mortification in this poem that reminds one of Propertius. Here is the same nervous restlessness, the same feverish exaltation. Ovid's revaluation of such concepts as *pudicitia*, *peccatum*, is doubtless intended seriously. If there are any traces of irony, it is bitter and harsh, bordering on sarcasm. 'Look at me,' the poet seems to cry, 'how great my love is! I have thrown overboard all my values in order to justify the errors of my beloved.' And in the same breath he deplores the deceptive comforts of self-pity.

At the beginning he had refused explicitly to judge Corinna by the traditional standards. Fickleness, he implied, is the privilege of beauty. Helen could not be both beautiful and faithful, he remarks elsewhere (*Heroides* 16.285ff); even the gods knew that and did not disapprove of her erotic adventures.

So far Ovid underlines his tolerance and generosity; he adds, however, that he does not want to have the truth forced down his throat. Corinna is free to deceive him as long as she does not *admit* her deceit. He actually wants her to do all the things that would hurt him if he knew them; he wants her to be disloyal to him and then, by denying what he knows, give him the opportunity to stage a supreme act of faith.

The double humiliation of being betrayed and told obvious lies, and still being able to forgive, this is the rigorous test from which his love will emerge more resplendent than ever. This game of make-believe has, at times, an almost painful effect on the modern reader because of the thoroughness with which it is carried through. It is a tragic situation, the situation of Verlaine's poem, *Lassitude*:

> *Mets ton front sur mon front et ta main dans ma main,*
> *Et fais-moi des serments que tu rompras demain . . .*

but in Ovid it loses its impact together with its simplicity.

The following three distichs (vv. 3-8) exhibit a few brilliant dialectical twists and turns – brilliant not because of any extraneous glitter, but because every thought is slowly turned by the poet to reveal its different aspects, and his language follows every turn. As often, Ovid's style owes its most striking effects to the stylistic devices of repetition and antithesis: *facias . . . facta*, *nocte . . . luce*, *latent . . . fateri*, *clam . . . palam*. But this technique never lapses into an agonized rhetoric; it is more play than conscious effort.

Non peccat quaecumque potest peccasse negare.

'she who can deny having sinned has not sinned.'

(v. 5)

This line suggests a rather unorthodox distinction between right and wrong. More than that, it implies an open criticism of something vaguely but piously called 'traditional values'. Sin is not defined as an objective fact; what counts is the spirit in which an act is committed.

Our poem in its position near the end of the *Amores* seems to indicate that it serves as a conclusion to the Corinna-romance. He does not avoid strong or even shocking images, such as v. 9f.

> *ignoto meretrix corpus iunctura Quiriti*
> *opposita populum summovet ante sera.*

'Even the prostitute who is ready to offer her body to an obscure citizen, locks the door first to keep out the crowd.'

Here the sordid physical reality corresponds to Corinna's sordidness in the moral sphere. Ovid wants to shock the reader. *Meretrix* is a rare word in Ovid, and so is *corpus iungere*, an expression which implies the mere animal union of two bodies, excluding any mutual attraction or sympathy. The prostitute in his comparison does not even bother to find out the name of the man whom she has just met on the street; still, she has more decency than Corinna. Although a courtesan of the lowest class, she has preserved a certain feeling of modesty, a feeling that Corinna has lost among the elegance and the fashionable frivolousness of the boudoirs.

What he actually wants her to do, the pattern of behaviour he prescribes for her, is this: 'Be reasonable and try at least to imitate the modest girls, and I might think you honest (though you are not)' (vv. 13-14). Let the heart be rotten, as long as the nice pretence is kept up. With his usual blithe spontaneousness, Ovid drafts an extraordinary revaluation of conventional 'good taste'. Such a theme lends itself best to a concise epigrammatic treatment. The paradox it implies could have been amusing or thought-provoking, but Ovid has stretched and twisted it until it ceases to be believable.

The next twelve lines (vv. 17-28) qualify the concept of *pudor* in an important sense. There is a place for 'naughtiness', *nequitia*, where *pudor* is not only superfluous, but unnecessary. It goes without saying that practically all of the *Amores* is based on this assumption. In an exquisitely rendered scene Ovid praises *nequitia*. How expressive these verbs are – *posuisse*, *sustinuisse*, *condatur*, *figuret*, *tremat* – how easily they fit into their place! As always Ovid has the right word at his fingertips. Effortlessly these vivid expressions pour forth, group themselves together with great ease, suggesting bright and animated pictures in a kind of shorthand.

A good deal of this art is routine, made up of stock phrases and self-variation. Still, the passage does not give the impression of having been pieced and pasted together laboriously. It is one of the secrets of Ovid's art that everything unfolds from a central theme, and he seems to say everything that can be said.

But Ovid returns almost immediately to his dialectical subtleties. He wants to enjoy a 'fool's belief', an attitude that is incompatible with the scepticism fashionable in Ovid's time. To assume, with a knowing smile, the worst about your fellow-man was a requirement of *savoir-vivre* in his society. He makes a strenuous but somewhat quixotic effort to return to a childlike state of blissful ignorance, to make love a great ordering power in his life, a power that triumphs over scepticism. But this effort is no less rational than the attitude it wishes to replace. Still it is possible to find a serious indictment of Ovid's society in this poem. 'We are incapable of true, unselfish devotion,' he seems to say. From this oppressive insight he escapes into a twilight world of make-believe. A wilful blindness appears to him as the only means of invigorating emotion and making it significant.

The theme has attracted other poets before Ovid. In a short elegy which probably belongs to his earliest period (3.20), Tibullus complains about the 'bitter rumours' of Glycera's disreputable conduct. Compared with Ovid's ill-concealed self-pity, Tibullus' complaint sounds refreshingly frank, almost a little clumsy. He praises the same kind of simple, natural life that Ovid seems to long for; and there, according to him, lies the solution, not in an artificially adopted attitude.

Like Ovid, Propertius (2.32) proclaims that a beautiful woman should be forgiven almost anything. For once he is more frivolous, less heavy-handed than Ovid. He seems proud of his open-mindedness. One has to be up-to-date, or rather, follow the gods and heroes of mythology. Ovid has omitted all this mythological apparatus; by focusing the reader's interest on his own person he gives the impression that a vital issue is at stake.

An elegy such as *Amores* 3.14 is the product of a narrow brilliant age, an age that dealt much in rumour, gossip and scandal because it had lost faith in the simple values of life. Throughout the poem one of these values, *pudor*, 'modesty', is discussed from various points of view. Unable to find a new meaning that might be acceptable to his contemporaries, the poet escapes into a philosophy of make-believe. It takes all of Ovid's ingenuity to breathe life into his paradoxical constructions. His effort is a little pathetic.

The social conditions of Ovid's time, as reflected in the *Amores*, are concrete enough. Funeral inscriptions such as the so-called *Laudatio Turiae* reveal the mutual tenderness on which a Roman marriage was based – but there was probably little room for romantic love. The love which Ovid celebrates can be found only within the loose relationship with a *domina*, 'mistress'. It is perfectly acceptable to talk about this kind of relationship. Marriage, however, is part of the private life of the individual, confined to his home, and should not be mentioned in public.

In the *Amores* this reality is overlaid with illusion. From the poet's point of view this means that he moves on more than one plane of reality. He sings of *amores* 'erotic situations (or adventures)', not of *amor*, 'love'. It goes without saying that both Ovid and his Corinna, who is not a 'prostitute', are capable of deep genuine emotion.

But what is Ovid trying to say? Does he want to convey a sense of the excitement and wonder he felt himself when he fell in love? Or is he fascinated by picturesque and amusing situations, brightly and effectively told? Or is it his ambition to compose startling new variations on the well-known themes? It is mainly the form, the presentation, that matters to him. He knows that he can make any story fresh and attractive. His themes, of course, are conventional; he likes to stress the typical elements of a situation, not its individual character. It seems that Ovid has finally exhausted the supply of these themes, characters and situations furnished by the tradition.

He is a virtuoso, but his virtuosity is the result of a fine, careless exuberance. He can absorb the external world and conjure up something highly coloured, sensuous and visually exciting. The history of Roman literature knows greater poets but no finer craftsman. To read the *Amores* provides the privilege of accompanying their author and protagonist on an infinitely entertaining pilgrimage of pleasure and good-natured self-deception.

Epilogue

The great period of the erotic elegy in Rome ends with Ovid's exile.

Love poetry was written at all times, and as it could not avoid the influence of the three elegists of the Augustan Age, much of it was in the elegiac form. Ovid's influence was strongest; he is followed by Tibullus and Propertius, in that order. Very little of this production is left. Instead of giving a list of all the elegiac poets from the end of the first century B.C. to the end of the sixth century A.D., I should like to mention only two authors, one pagan, the other Christian.

Maximian lived in an age of turmoil, when Italy was torn apart by the struggle between Byzantium and the Goths. His six elegies celebrate a violent, sensual kind of love. Among the women he claims to have loved, one is called Lycoris, like the mistress of Cornelius Gallus; other pseudonyms found in his poems are Candida, Aquilina and 'the Greek girl'. Some of the passionate scenes which he describes in great detail, may be the product of his overheated imagination. One sees him as an ageing Casanova who rehearses the erotic experiences of his youth and tries to recapture pleasures that are lost forever. There is something morbid and grotesque about the juvenile day-dreams of an old man. In the third elegy, an unexpected praise of *virginitas* introduces a Christian ideal into this unashamedly pagan poetry that owes as much to the *Priapea* as to the classical love-elegy.

The Christian poets read the Augustan elegists and adapted whole lines to their new context. The worldly Eros is transformed into the Christian Agape, the enjoyment of the here and now replaced by the necessity of *vivere deo*. When Agnes, the spiritual daughter of St Radegund, was made abbess of Poitiers, Venantius Fortunatus (530–600 A.D.) wrote an elegy in her honour (c. 8.3). This poem contains the love letter of a nun addressed to Christ, a Christian version of Ovid's *Heroides* (vv. 227-248). The nun takes the place of, say, Laodamia, and Christ, the absent lover, that of Protesilaus. He receives the letter in heaven and reads it aloud to the celestial assembly, the Christian counterpart to the *concilium deorum*.[1]

[1] Cf. Wolfgang Schmid, 'Ein christlicher Heroidenbrief des 6. Jh.': *Studien zur Textgeschichte und Textkritik*, hrsg. v. H. Dahlmann u. R. Merkelbach (1959), p. 253ff and the same author in: *Reallexikon für Antike und Christentum* 4 (1959), col. 1059.

Bibliography

This bibliography is by no means exhaustive. It contains only the books and articles to which I feel particularly indebted. Many more could be listed (a few are mentioned here and there in the notes). For a complete survey of the work done on the Latin elegiac poets during the last forty years or so, see J. Marouzeau, *L'Année Philologique*, published yearly, under 'Ovidius', 'Propertius', 'Tibullus' and, in the second part of each volume, under 'Poésie'.

A critical report on the work done after 1937 and before 1952 will be found in K. Büchner, *Lateinische Literatur und Sprache in der Forschung seit 1937* (Bern 1951). In 1953 the second volume of the *Entretiens sur l'Antiquité Classique*, sponsored by the Baron Hardt (Vandœuvres-Genève) was published. It deals with the Greek influence on Latin poetry from Catullus to Ovid and contains lectures by J. Bayet, A. Rostagni, V. Pöschl, F. Klingner, P. Boyancé and L. P. Wilkinson, each lecture being followed by the record of an oral discussion – a very stimulating approach to many of the problems dealt with in the present book.

Occasionally, I refer in the notes to Pauly-Wissowa-Kroll, *Real-Encyclopädie der classischen Altertumswissenschaft* (abbreviated: RE).

(1) GENERAL: GREEK ELEGY

L. ALFONSI and W. SCHMID, Article 'Elegie' in: *Reallexikon für Antike und Christentum* 4 (1959), 1026ff.

P. FRIEDLÄNDER and H. B. HOFFLEIT, *Epigrammata* (Univ. of Calif. Press 1948).

H. HERTER, Article 'Kallimachos' in: RE Suppl. 5, 386ff.

H. HERTER, Bibliographical report on Callimachus in: *Bursians Jahresberichte* 255 (1937), 157ff.

E. HOWALD and E. STAIGER, *Kallimachos* (Zürich 1955). Selection of texts with German translations and introduction.

R. PFEIFFER (ed.), *Callimachus*, 2 vols. (Oxford 1949 and 1953).

U. V. WILAMOWITZ-MOELLENDORFF, *Hellenistische Dichtung*, 2 vols. (Berlin 1924).

(2) LATIN ELEGY, ORIGINS AND CHARACTER

Critical edition of Catullus by R. A. B. Mynors (Oxford 1959).
Commentary by C. J. Fordyce (Oxford 1961).

English translation by H. Gregory (London 1956).

E. BURCK, 'Römische Wesenszüge in der augusteischen Liebeselegie', in: *Hermes* (1952), 163ff.

A. GUILLEMIN, 'L'élément humain dans l'élégie latine', in: *Revue des Études Latines* (1940), 95ff.

G. HIGHET, *Poets in a Landscape* (New York, 1957); on the German translation (Munich 1964) cf. G. Luck, in: *Gnomon* (1965), 625.

E. HOWALD, *Das Wesen der lateinischen Dichtung* (Zürich 1948).

F. JACOBY, 'Zur Entstehung der römischen Elegie', in: *Rheinisches Museum* (1905), 38ff.

G. LAFAYE, *Catulle et ses modèles* (Paris 1894); cf. J. Girard, in: *Journal des Savants* (1894), 533ff; 637ff.

E. LÖFSTEDT, 'Aspects of the History of Roman Love-Poetry', in: *Roman Literary Portraits*, transl. by P. M. Fraser (Oxford 1958).

R. PICHON, *De sermone amatorio apud Latinos elegiarum scriptores* (Paris 1902).

W. Y. SELLAR, *Horace and the Elegiac Poets*, 2nd ed. (Oxford 1899).

(3) Corpus Tibullianum

Critical edition with bibliography by F. W. Lenz (Leiden 1964); cf. H. D. Jocelyn, in: *Gnomon* (1966), 35ff.

Commentaries by Heyne-Wunderlich, 4th ed. (1817) and K. F. Smith (New York 1913; repr. Darmstadt 1964). On Book 1 only by J. André (Paris 1963).

Concordance by E. N. O'Neil (Ithaca, N.Y. 1963).

English translation by J. P. Postgate (Loeb Class. Libr.).

German translation of Books 1 and 2 by G. Luck (Zürich 1964).

Selections: J. P. Postgate (London 1922).

J. P. ELDER, 'Tibullus: tersus atque elegans', in: *Critical Essays on Roman Literature. Elegy and Lyric*. Ed. by J. P. Sullivan (London 1962), 65ff.

F. LEO, 'Ueber einige Elegien Tibulls', in: *Philol. Untersuchungen* 2 (1881), 1ff.

F. SOLMSEN, 'Tibullus as an Augustan Poet', in: *Hermes* (1962), 295ff.

W. STEIDLE, 'Das Motiv der Lebenswahl bei Tibull und Properz', in: *Wiener Studien* (1962), 100ff.

(4) Propertius

Critical edition by E. A. Barber (Oxford 1953).

Commentaries by H. E. Butler and E. A. Barber (Oxford 1933), and by W. A. Camps (Cambridge 1961ff).

Selections: J. P. Postgate, 2nd ed. (London 1884).

English translations by H. E. Butler (Loeb Class. Libr.) and A. E. Watts (London 1961).

German translation by G. Luck (Zürich 1964).

Spanish translation by A. Tovar and M. T. Belfiore Mártire (Barcelona 1963).

Index verborum by J. S. Phillimore (Oxford 1911).

Textual criticism: D. R. Shackleton Bailey, *Propertiana*, 2nd ed. (Cambridge 1968); G. P. Goold, 'Noctes Propertianae', in: *Harv. Stud. Class. Philol.* (1967), 59ff.

J. P. BOUCHER, *Études sur Properce* (Paris 1965).

F. SOLMSEN, 'Propertius in his literary relations with Tibullus and Vergil', in: *Philologus* (1961), 273ff.

H. TRÄNKLE, *Die Sprachkunst des Properz und die Tradition der lateinischen Dichtersprache* (Hermes Einzelschriften, 1960).

W. WILI, 'Die literarischen Beziehungen des Properz zu Horaz', in: *Festschrift Tièche* (Bern 1947), 181ff.

(5) OVID

Critical edition of the *Amores* by F. Munari, with Italian translation, 3rd ed. (Florence 1959); of the *Carmina Amatoria* by E. J. Kenney (Oxford 1961); cf. G. Luck, in: *Gnomon* (1963), 156ff; G. P. Goold, in: *Harv. Stud. Class. Philol.* (1965), 1ff.

Index verborum, in: Burman's edition (Amsterdam 1727).

Concordance by R. J. Deferrari and others (Washington, D.C. 1939).

Commentary on the *Amores* by P. Brandt (1911).

English translation by A. G. Lee (London 1968).

German translation by R. Harder and W. Marg, 2nd ed. (Munich 1962).

Collection of essays and articles, ed. by M. v. Albrecht and E. Zinn (Darmstadt 1968).

H. FRÄNKEL, *Ovid: A Poet Between Two Worlds* 2nd ed. (Univ. of Calif. Press 1956).

W. KRAUS, Article 'Ovid', in: RE²18.1910ff (reprinted, with changes, in the collection of essays mentioned above).

A. G. LEE, 'Tenerorum lusor amorum', in: *Critical Essays* (quoted above, under Tibullus), 149ff.

E. K. RAND, *Ovid and His Influence* (Our Debt to Greece and Rome, London 1926).

L. P. WILKINSON, *Ovid Recalled* (Cambridge 1955). Abridgement: *Ovid Surveyed* (Cambridge 1962).

Index

(3) WORDS AND IDEAS